S0-CYD-647

Jane Austen

Pocket **BIOGRAPHIES**

Jane Austen

HELEN LEFROY

SUTTON PUBLISHING

First published in 1997 by
Sutton Publishing Limited · Phoenix Mill
Thrupp · Stroud · Gloucestershire · GL5 2BU

Copyright © Helen Lefroy, 1997

All rights reserved. No part of this publication may be
reproduced, stored in a retrieval system, or transmitted,
in any form, or by any means, electronic, mechanical,
photocopying, recording or otherwise, without the
prior permission of the publisher and copyright holder.

The author has asserted the moral right to be identified
as the author of this work.

British Library Cataloguing in Publication Data
A catalogue record for this book is available from the
British Library

ISBN 0-7509-1580-3

ALAN SUTTON™ and SUTTON™ are the
trade marks of Sutton Publishing Limited

Typeset in 13/18 pt Perpetua.
Typesetting and origination by
Sutton Publishing Limited.
Printed in Great Britain by
The Guernsey Press Company Limited,
Guernsey, Channel Islands.

With gratitude for memories of Jane Austen's great-great-nieces, my godmother Louisa Langlois Lefroy and her sisters, Cousin Jessie and Cousin Isabel

C O N T E N T S

CHRONOLOGY

1764	The Revd George Austen and Cassandra Leigh married in Walcot Church, Bath
1765	James, their first child, born
1766	George, the handicapped son, born
1767	Edward born; he took the name Knight in 1812
1768	The Austens move into Steventon Rectory
1771	Henry Thomas born
1773	Cassandra Elizabeth born
1774	Francis (Frank) William born
1775	16 December, Jane born
1779	Charles John, the Austens' last child, born
1783	Cassandra, Jane and their cousin Jane Cooper go to Mrs Cawley in Oxford for lessons
1784–8	Amateur dramatics at Steventon Rectory
1785	Cassandra and Jane join Jane Cooper at the Abbey School, Reading, but return home at the end of 1786
1787–93	Jane busy writing stories and sketches
1791	Edward marries Elizabeth Bridges

1792	James marries Anne Mathew
	Cassandra becomes engaged to the
	Revd Tom Fowle
1795	James's wife Anne dies; his daughter
	Anna is taken to live at Steventon
	Rectory
1795–6	Tom Lefroy in Hampshire for Christmas
	and New Year.
	Jane begins writing 'First Impressions',
	the first draft of *Pride and Prejudice*
1797	Mr Austen writes to a London publisher
	offering to send the manuscript of 'First
	Impressions'; the offer is refused
	Tom Fowle dies of yellow fever in the
	West Indies
1799	Mrs Leigh Perrot (Mrs Austen's sister-
	in-law) charged with larceny and
	committed to gaol
1800	Mrs Leigh Perrot tried and acquitted
1801	Mr and Mrs Austen, Cassandra and Jane
	move to Bath
1802	In December Harris Bigg Wither
	proposes to Jane; he is accepted but
	turned down next morning
1803	Copyright of 'Susan' (*Northanger Abbey*)
	sold to publisher for £10.
	The Austens holiday in Lyme Regis
1804	Jane's friend Mrs Lefroy is killed after a
	fall from her horse
1805	Death of Mr Austen

Chronology

1806	The Austens leave Bath, and after a round of visits join Frank and his bride in Southampton
1809	Mrs Austen, Cassandra, Jane and Martha Lloyd move to Chawton in Hampshire
1811	Jane at work on *Mansfield Park* *Sense and Sensibility* published
1813	*Pride and Prejudice* published
1814	Jane begins writing *Emma* *Mansfield Park* published
1815	Jane begins writing *Persuasion* Jane is invited to see round Carlton House, the Prince Regent's London house, and to dedicate to him her next novel – *Emma* – published in December
1816	Henry negotiates purchase of manuscript of 'Susan' from dilatory publisher; it is published posthumously as *Northanger Abbey*
1817	Jane begins writing *Sanditon*, but manuscript remains uncompleted In May Cassandra takes Jane to Winchester for medical help 18 July, Jane Austen dies; she is buried in Winchester Cathedral on 24 July December, *Northanger Abbey* and *Persuasion* published together in four volumes, with a 'Biographical Notice' of the author by Henry Austen

INTRODUCTION

Jane Austen (1775–1817) wrote only six complete novels, two of which were published after her death. In these novels the life of the gentry, land-owners and clergy at the end of the eighteenth and the early part of the nineteenth centuries is shown in detail. They are peopled by an assembly of characters, men and women, old and young – some, but not many, children – who are unforgettable and can become as real to the reader as his or her own friends and family. Jane Austen did not step outside her own self-imposed limits. She does not write of titled people in grand houses – although she knew the aristocratic families living in the corner of North Hampshire where she lived with her parents for her first twenty-five years, and as a young and attractive girl was invited to the annual balls given by titled families.

Critics accuse Jane Austen of being obsessed with money and rich relations. But both were a necessity in the society to which she belonged. As the younger daughter of a country parson she knew from an early age that without a dowry she would be unlikely to find a husband among her circle of friends. An eldest son would inherit the property and money to keep it together, or he might be lucky and marry a rich wife. What became of younger sons? They entered the church, the armed forces, and the law; not until later in the nineteenth century did they engage in trade. As benefices in the Church of England were largely privately owned or the property of university colleges, it was essential to know or be related to owners of advowsons and rectories. Twice Mr Austen sought to advance the careers of his two naval sons, both of them reliable, enthusiastic and thoroughly professional young officers, by invoking the help of friends in high places.

All Jane Austen's work shows a recognizable standard of values. Her father was a country vicar; his family remained faithful Christians throughout their lives, and went regularly to church. Jane took for granted that a person should be sincere, unselfish, disinterested and unworldly, and that virtue should be judged by good sense and good taste. These beliefs are fundamental to her work. In *Sense and Sensibility*, the first of her novels to be published, the impetuous

Marianne, who judges by the heart, is contrasted with her sister Elinor who believes that the heart should be disciplined by good sense and moral principle. Marianne is of course far more attractive a character than Elinor – and should not have been paired off at the end of the book with Colonel Brandon! *Pride and Prejudice* shows the foolishness of trusting to first impressions which are corrected by understanding and reflection. Emma (in *Emma*) is over-confident and tries to manage the lives of others without pausing to understand their characters, or even her own.

Jane and her elder sister Cassandra were insepar-able friends from childhood. It is from Jane's letters to Cassandra, written whenever they were away from each other, that one learns the details of their everyday life: the price of muslin, the arrival of yet more nephews and nieces, and the state of their mother's health. All these details are interspersed with comments kind and cruel about friends, relations and strangers. Jane Austen's interest revolved around people – their eccentricities, appearance and dialogue. From them she created the characters which give her novels universal and lasting appeal.

STEVENTON – THE EARLY YEARS

For generations Austens had lived at Horsmonden in Kent, where they were engaged in the woollen industry. At the end of the seventeenth century John Austen, owner of the family property, married a remarkably strong and determined woman, Elizabeth Weller. Widowed in 1704, and with a string of debts and children, she took on the job of housekeeper at Sevenoaks Grammar School and also lodged the Master. As funds were only available for her eldest son to go to university, the younger boys were obliged to seek apprenticeships. Francis became a prosperous lawyer in Sevenoaks and William a surgeon in Tonbridge. William – Jane's grandfather – died when his son George (1731–1805) was six years old. From 1741 to 1747 George Austen – Jane's father – attended Tonbridge School. An equable temperament, firm character and ability to work hard enabled him to take up the scholarship to St John's College, Oxford, reserved for a boy from Tonbridge School. After taking his degree the Tonbridge connection enabled him to stay on at St John's for a further seven years, studying divinity.

He was ordained a priest in the Church of England; he returned to Kent to take up the job of second master at his old school, and at the same time to be perpetual curate at Shipbourne, a few miles away. Three years later he went back to his Oxford college as assistant chaplain. As a bachelor he could remain at St John's indefinitely but with no financial resources of his own, if he wished to marry he must find a benefice rich enough to support a family. A female second cousin had married Thomas Knight, the owner of the estate of Godmersham in Kent, who then had the good fortune to inherit more property and land in Hampshire, at Steventon and Chawton. Thomas Knight was able to offer the benefice of Steventon to George Austen. George's wealthy uncle Francis purchased two more benefices in parishes near Steventon: George could have whichever became available first. So with the prospect of a tolerable income from two parishes,

George set out to woo and to win the heart of Cassandra Leigh, younger daughter of the Revd Thomas Leigh of Harpsden, near Henley-on-Thames.

Cassandra came from the Gloucestershire family of Leigh, who were descended from Sir Thomas Leigh, Lord Mayor of London in the time of Elizabeth I. Wealthy and powerful, he acquired the enormous mansion and surrounding lands of Stoneleigh Abbey. As a reward for welcoming Charles I to the Abbey during the Civil War, Thomas Leigh's son was given a peerage.

George Austen and Cassandra Leigh were married at Walcot Church, Bath, on 26 April 1764. They set off immediately for Hampshire, but as the rectory at Steventon was in poor condition, they spent the first four years of their married life a couple of miles away at Deane Rectory, where their first three sons were born: James (1765), George (1766) and Edward (1767). George was born handicapped and did not live at home but was cared for in a village in the neighbourhood until his death at the age of seventy-two.

Steventon Rectory stood at the foot of the lane

which leads up to the simple medieval church of St Nicholas. There were three main rooms on the ground floor at the front, with George Austen's study and library at the back; above were seven bedrooms and three attics. The house was demolished in 1826; all that remains is a pump in the corner of a field. Steventon is still a small rural village, surrounded by fields and woods, in a valley between two main roads. The Austens would have walked or ridden a few miles north to Deane Gate to pick up a stage-coach to London, or to Andover, Salisbury and the west. A few miles to the south was the Wheatsheaf Inn, a regular stopping place for coaches from Winchester and Southampton en route to London, where the horses could be changed and passengers given just twenty minutes for breakfast.

At Steventon the Austen family was enlarged: Henry (1771), Cassandra (1773), Frank (1774), Jane (16 December 1775) and finally Charles (1779) were all born there. To supplement his income George Austen decided to take pupils, the sons of the local gentry, who were educated with his own boys and were boarded in the house. With the help of a bailiff George Austen cultivated his three acres of glebe land, and a further 200 acres which he rented.

Jane had the great good fortune to be born into a supremely happy and resourceful family. Her parents were never wealthy but both had aristocratic connections. Parsons on the whole were better educated than squires, and had a recognized and respected place in society. A degree from Oxford or Cambridge University was the only essential requirement for ordination in the Church of England.

Cassandra Austen, a lively, intelligent wife and mother, was a thrifty and sensible manager of her large family. She kept a few cows at Steventon and would certainly have had a well-stocked poultry-yard. To add variety to meals for the family and visitors she and her husband worked hard in the vegetable garden and orchard. She was a great reader of novels, borrowed from a circulating library in Basingstoke, and she had a gift for writing verse and choosing words to rhyme – a gift inherited by several of her children. A grand-daughter later remembered that visitors to Steventon Rectory would usually find her in the front parlour with a needle in her hand, making and mending.

Cassandra Austen's sister Jane had married the Revd Dr Edward Cooper in 1768. He gave up a fellowship at All Souls College, Oxford, to become the rector of a parish near Bath. Their two children, Edward and Jane, were good friends of the Austen family. When the Austens decided that their elder daughter Cassandra should join her cousin Jane Cooper to be given lessons by Mrs Cawley at Oxford, Jane Austen, then aged seven, insisted on going too. Mrs Cawley, the childless widow of a former head of an Oxford college, was strict and unsympathetic. She took the three girls with her when she moved to Southampton. There the Austen girls caught typhus. Jane was seriously ill and it was only Jane Cooper's presence of mind in writing to the Austens at Steventon which saved the girls. Mrs Austen and Mrs Cooper rescued their daughters in time, but Mrs Cooper caught typhus and died.

Cassandra and Jane now spent more than a year at home, but by 1785 it was time for Cassandra, the elder girl, to receive more education. In a household of boys and young men it may have been thought she should have the opportunity to acquire the feminine accomplishments of music, dancing and needlework. Again Jane insisted on accom-

panying her sister, which prompted her mother's
comment that, 'if Cassandra's head had been going
to be cut off, Jane would have hers cut off too'.[1]
Now aged twelve and nine, Cassandra and Jane
joined Jane Cooper at the Abbey School, Reading. It
seems to have been a happy establishment, with
lessons in the morning only. But Mr Austen would
have to pay fees of £35 per annum for each girl;
these may have been more than George Austen
could afford. In the following years he would also
need to find fees of £25 a year for his son Frank
when he entered the Naval Academy at Portsmouth,
though extras (the barber, shoemaker, instruments
and stationery, for example) brought the total cost
of maintaining a boy at the Academy nearer to £50 a
year. So after only eighteen months the girls
returned home. From then on Jane educated herself
from the resources of her father's extensive library,
and certainly with his guidance.

The close friendship between the sisters was
remembered many years later by their niece Anna:

> Their sisterly affection for each other could hardly be
> exceeded. . . . This attachment was never interrupted
> or weakened. They lived in the same home, and

shared the same bed-room, till separated by death. . . .
Cassandra's was the colder and calmer disposition;
she was always prudent and well judging, but with
less outward demonstration of feeling and less
sunniness of temper than Jane possessed. . . .
Cassandra had the *merit* of having her temper always
under command; Jane had the *happiness* of a temper
that never required to be commanded.[2]

In 1792 Mr Austen's niece Eliza de Feuillide wrote
of the sisters: 'Cassandra & Jane are both very much
grown (the latter is now taller than myself) and
greatly improved as well in Manners as in Person. . . .
They are I think equally sensible, and both so to a
degree seldom met with, but still My Heart gives
the preference to Jane, whose kind partiality to me,
indeed requires a return of the same nature.'[3]

After Jane's death in 1817 Henry Austen wrote of
his sister: 'Her carriage and deportment were quiet,
yet graceful. Her features were separately good.
Their assemblage produced an unrivalled expression
of that cheerfulness, sensibility, and benevolence,
which were her real characteristics. Her complexion was of the finest texture. . . . Her voice was
extremely sweet.'[4]

And in 1870, when he came to write *A Memoir of*

Jane Austen, her nephew Edward said of his aunt: 'In person she was very attractive; her figure was rather tall and slender, her step light and firm, and her whole appearance expressive of health and animation. In complexion she was a clear brunette with a rich colour; she had full round cheeks, with mouth and nose small and well formed, bright hazel eyes, and brown hair forming natural curls close round her face.'[5]

Life at Steventon in 1786 was not dull. The good-looking and lively brothers were popular, and always ready to join friends for a day's hunting or rough shooting. James, the eldest, was especially keen on the craze for amateur theatricals, and for several years would persuade his brothers and their friends to join in performing plays or a pantomime either in the house or the barn. The cast was occasionally joined by George Austen's niece Eliza de Feuillide. Married to a French army officer (who was later guillotined) she came to England for the birth of their son. Jane was fascinated by this pretty, sophisticated cousin, her sharp eyes missing nothing as Eliza teased and flirted with the susceptible James and Henry Austen.

At the age of about twelve, Jane began to write down some of the stories she had probably told Cassandra in the bedroom they shared. She copied the stories into three manuscript books which she labelled 'Volume the First', 'Volume the Second' and 'Volume the Third'. They are known collectively as the *Juvenilia*. The stories are light-hearted, witty and amusing, and would have been read aloud to the family in the evenings. 'She also had a high-spirited taste for nonsense. . . . At fifteen her writing is already marked by her characteristic neat stylishness, her crisp irony.'[6]

The brothers now began to leave home. Edward, after travelling on the Continent, was spending more time with Mr and Mrs Thomas Knight who had chosen him to be their heir. He was the first of the brothers to marry, his bride being Elizabeth Bridges, a beautiful girl from Kent. He was a generous and genial host, always welcoming family and friends to Godmersham Park, the fine country house near Ashford in Kent later bequeathed to him by the Knights. The second house he inherited was at Chawton in Hampshire. Cassandra was frequently called on to run the household, and to amuse the children whenever Elizabeth was lying in, usually for a month, after the birth of another child. She was there when Elizabeth died unexpectedly after the arrival of Brook John in 1808.

Frank had also left the rectory. After two years at the Royal Naval Academy, his first sea-going appointment took him to the East Indies for four years. In 1791 Jane's youngest brother Charles followed Frank to the Naval Academy.

Now ordained, the eldest brother James acted as curate in neighbouring parishes. In 1792 he married Anne Mathew. They began their married life at Deane Rectory, just as his parents had done. There Anna was born, but two years later her mother died suddenly. The motherless little girl was taken to live at Steventon Rectory with her grandparents and two aunts, and thus were forged the strong ties of affection and understanding which were often much tested when Anna became a headstrong, undisciplined teenager.

Two years later, after hesitating between two girls named Mary, James married Mary Lloyd, his sisters' good friend. Mrs Austen wrote her a warm letter of welcome: 'Mr Austen and Myself desire you will accept our best Love, and that you will believe us truly sincere when we assure you that we feel the most heartfelt satisfaction at the prospect we have of adding you to the number of our very good Children.'[7] James and Mary had two children: James Edward, and seven years later, Caroline. Sadly, Mary was never able to make Anna feel wanted and a part of the family.

Jane's favourite brother Henry had followed James to Oxford, and could have chosen to be ordained. However, in 1793 France and England were at war and this may have prompted Henry to purchase a commission in the Oxfordshire Regiment of Militia. He served as an army officer for the next eight years. After dallying for two years, the fascinating Eliza de Feuillide, now a widow, agreed to marry Henry. For four years she and her son followed the drum. When Henry became a banker and an army agent in London Eliza was a delightful and welcoming hostess to friends and family. Sadly this enchanting cousin died after a long illness. Jane was with her for the last few days.

In 1792 Jane Cooper, who had been at school with Cassandra and Jane, was welcomed to the rectory by her aunt, Mrs Austen. Her father had died and she was on her own. A few months later she was married in Steventon Church to an able naval officer. Mr Austen's former pupil, Tom Fowle, recently ordained, took the service, and later found an opportunity to propose to Cassandra. While waiting for a vacant living he agreed to accompany his kinsman Lord Craven as his private chaplain on a military expedition to the West Indies. He hoped to be rewarded with a lucrative benefice in Shropshire in Lord Craven's gift. The following year came news that 'her dear and only love' had died of yellow fever in St Domingo.

Cassandra folded the wedding garments away and devoted herself henceforward to her family and to the increasing number of nephews and nieces. She never married.

T W O

STEVENTON – THE LATER YEARS

At Steventon Rectory there can have been little fear of isolation from the momentous events in Europe and in America. The American War of Independence had ended in 1783, but in 1793 France declared war on England. The two naval brothers were involved in fighting the French at sea, Henry was serving as an officer in the Oxfordshire Militia, and Eliza de Feuillide's husband had been guillotined. Newspapers were expensive in those days and tended to be shared between households. Mr Holder of Ashe Park, who had acquired a fortune in the West Indies, used to pass on his copy of the *Hampshire Chronicle* to the Austens. Its closely packed columns would be eagerly read at the Rectory – first the movements of ships, then news from London and Europe, agricultural prices and perhaps the advertisements.

The *Chronicle* liked to keep its readers informed of death and disaster among the high- and lowly-born. In 1788, when Jane was twelve, Thomas Twisleton, Lord Saye and Sele, who had married one of Mrs Austen's second cousins, cut his throat with a razor and stabbed himself with a sword at his house in Harley Street, London. A few months later his eighteen-year-old son eloped to Gretna Green with a minor, a young girl he had met while they were both acting in amateur theatricals. Perhaps it is not surprising that neither Cassandra nor Jane were given parts in the amateur theatricals at Steventon.

This story is echoed in *Mansfield Park* (1814). After rehearsing *Lovers' Vows* in Sir Thomas Bertram's absence, both his daughters get entangled with the actors: Julia elopes to Scotland with Mr Yates 'who had not much to recommend him beyond habits of fashion and expense'. This was found to be a less desperate business than it had at first appeared. Julia was humble and wished to be forgiven, Mr Yates was desirous of being received into the family. 'He was not very solid; but there was a hope of his becoming less trifling – of his being at least tolerably domestic and quiet; and, at any rate, there was comfort in finding his estate rather more, and his debts much less, than he had feared.'[1] Julia's married sister was less fortunate. The man she eloped with soon threw her over and her husband refused to have her back.

Tales of debauchery, heavy drinking and extravagance echoed round the neighbourhood of Steventon when the Prince Regent rented Kempshot Park, near Basingstoke, for a few years to use as a hunting lodge. Mrs Fitzherbert, the mistress whom he had married illegally in 1785, super-intended decorations in the main rooms and the layout of the garden. Lacking a legitimate heir, the Prince Regent bigamously married Princess Caroline of Brunswick in 1795 and brought her to Kempshot for a few riotous days of honeymoon.[2] Then the royal party left and did not return. Jane's brother James probably met the Prince and his friends in the hunting field.

Cassandra and Jane had grown into attractive and lively young women and were popular guests at private parties, Assembly Room dances and country house balls. There they would meet their friends and the usual string of dancing partners. At Christmas 1795 a good-looking stranger appeared. Tom Lefroy was the nineteen-year-old nephew of the Revd George Lefroy, of the rectory at Ashe, a few miles north of Steventon. His wife Anne had known Jane Austen since childhood, and despite a difference of twenty-five years in their ages, they had a special affection for one another. Jane probably enjoyed visiting Ashe Rectory, so different from her own male-dominated home where her mother was preoccupied with the cares of house-keeping, her dairy and the garden.

George Lefroy had remodelled the small rectory at Ashe to make it a pleasant country house. His wife was elegant and warm-hearted, 'a remarkable person. Her rare endowments of goodness, talents, graceful person, and engaging manners, were sufficient to secure her a prominent place in any society into which she was thrown; while her enthusiastic eagerness of disposition rendered her especially attractive to a clever and lively girl.'[3] At Ashe she welcomed a stream of visitors. While her husband preferred to stay at home, she and her guests, or young friends like the Austen girls, would set off in the carriage for an evening party. After supper the carpet would be rolled back, someone would play the fiddle or pianoforte, and six or eight couples would enjoy impromptu dancing. Meanwhile the coachman would be entertained below stairs, the horse resting or munching hay in the stable, until a bright moon lighted the road home, often after midnight.

Jane gave her sister a long account of a ball at which she had clearly flouted convention by dancing too frequently with Tom Lefroy:

> You scold me so much in the nice long letter which I have this moment received from you, that I am almost afraid to tell you how my Irish friend and I behaved. . . . He is a very gentlemanlike, good-looking, pleasant young man, I assure you. But as to our ever having met, except at the three last balls, I cannot say much; for he is so excessively laughed at about me at Ashe, that he is ashamed of coming to Steventon, and ran away when we called on Mrs Lefroy a few days ago.[4]

The Lefroy children — Lucy, aged seventeen, George, fourteen, and Edward, eleven — were probably the teasers. Ben, aged four-and-a-half, was too young to join in.

Some months after Tom left Hampshire in January 1796 to study law in London, Jane began work on the first version of *Pride and Prejudice*, which she called 'First Impressions'. She read it aloud to her family and it so impressed her father that he wrote to Thomas Cadell, a London publisher, offering to send the manuscript. He also asked what the cost would be for publishing at the author's expense, and what the publisher would offer by way of payment if the manuscript was accepted for publication. Across the top of the letter is written 'declined by Return of post'. This rejection remains a cautionary tale for all publishers, though it is true that Thomas Cadell himself had not seen or read the manuscript.

Undeterred, Jane began revising another manuscript, provisionally entitled 'Elinor and Marianne', and written in the form of letters. But she found this too restricting and later transformed the text into *Sense and Sensibility*, the first of her books to be published, in 1811.

As their parents were able to manage at Steventon Rectory quite happily, Cassandra and Jane were free to go and stay with relations and friends. Returning to Steventon after one visit to Mrs Lloyd, Jane was greeted by her mother with the startling news that they were going to live in Bath.

THREE

BATH

In 1800, at the age of seventy, George Austen decided to retire and hand over his parish duties to his son James; his decision to move to Bath is said to have come as a great shock to Jane. Later Jane's feelings changed and she wrote to Cassandra: 'I get more & more reconciled to the idea of our removal. We have lived long enough in this Neighbourhood, the Basingstoke Balls are certainly on the decline, there is something interesting in the bustle of going away, & the prospect of spending future summers by the Sea or in Wales is very delightful.'[1] She was deeply attached to her home, to the Hampshire countryside and to many friends in the neighbourhood. Her happy, carefree way of life was about to end. Before the move, furniture and livestock had to be sold. This included George Austen's library of 500 books and Jane's piano. The Austens had now to budget carefully. 'The trouble & risk of the removal would be more than the advantage of having them at a place, where everything may be purchased.'[2]

The city of Bath lies in a hollow, with the River Avon winding through it, and the once wooded hillsides have been covered with buildings. In an age of elegance the city was developed by men of genius: Ralph Allen, and John Wood, father and son. Using the golden stone from local quarries, they built streets, squares and the incomparable Royal Crescent and the Circus.

Some thirty years before the Austens moved there, Tobias Smollett had given this description of the city in *Humphry Clinker* (1771):

Bath to me is a new world. All is gaiety, good humour, and diversion. The eye is continually entertained with the splendour of dress and equipage, and the ear with the sound of coaches, chaises, chairs and other carriages. The merry bells ring round from morn till night. We have music in the Pump Room every morning, cotillions every forenoon in the rooms, balls twice a week, and concerts every other night, besides private assemblies and parties without number.

He continues with a description of the public rooms

– the Upper and the Lower – where the company met on alternate evenings:

> They are spacious, lofty, and when lighted up appear very striking. They are generally crowded with well-dressed people, who drink tea in separate parties, play at cards, walk, or sit and chat together. Twice a week there is a ball, the expense of which is defrayed among the gentlemen, and every subscriber has three tickets.

By the end of the century, when the Austens arrived, Bath's heyday was over. Now retired clergymen, elderly lawyers and admirals were brought in sedan chairs to the Pump Room to drink the waters to cure gout and rheumatics; they then strolled to the Assembly Rooms for staid music and dancing. As Jane Austen wrote:

> The worst of Bath was the number of its plain women. He [Sir Walter Elliot] did not mean to say that there were no pretty women, but the number of the plain was out of all proportion. He had frequently observed, as he walked, that one handsome face would be followed by thirty, or five-and-thirty frights; and once, as he had stood in a shop in Bond Street, he had counted eighty-seven women go by,

one after another, without there being a tolerable face among them. It had been a frosty morning, to be sure, a sharp frost, which hardly one woman in a thousand could stand the test of. But still, there certainly were a dreadful multitude of ugly women in Bath; and as for the men! they were infinitely worse.[3]

In May 1801 Mrs Austen and Jane went on ahead to search for a suitable, affordable house to rent. They stayed with Mrs Austen's brother James Leigh Perrot and his wife, and inspected several properties. By the time George Austen and Cassandra arrived, 4 Sydney Place had become available. They took a three-year lease, and it became their home until shortly before George Austen's death in January 1805. At some distance from the more fashionable part of the city, for the Austens it had the advantage of facing on to Sydney Gardens, a public space where they could stroll freely, and which was enlivened on summer evenings by illuminations and firework displays. Beyond was open countryside.

The house had only recently been built, and the full length of the terrace had yet to be completed. After being shown round the house in 1901, Constance Hill wrote:

We have . . . sat in the pretty drawing-room with its three tall windows overlooking the Gardens. . . . The house is roomy and commodious. Beneath the drawing-room, which is on the first floor, are the dining-room and arched hall from which a passage leads to a garden at the back of the house. The large, old-fashioned kitchen, with its shining copper pans and its dresser, laden with fine old china, looked as if it had remained untouched since the Austens' day.[4]

The Austens had visited Bath twice previously. In 1797 Mrs Austen had been unwell and accepted her brother's invitation to spend a few weeks at the Leigh Perrots' house in The Paragon, a short distance from Walcot Church where she had been married thirty years earlier. Cassandra, Jane and their mother were fetched from Steventon by James Leigh Perrot in his carriage as he travelled to Bath from his other house, Scarlets, near Twyford in Berkshire.

Two years later Jane and her mother went again to Bath, this time joining Edward, Elizabeth and their two eldest children. Edward had been unwell and hoped to be cured by the spa waters. The journey from Steventon took two days, the party stopping for the night at an inn in Devizes where they dined on lobster and asparagus. 'Our Journey yesterday went off exceedingly well; nothing occurred to alarm or delay us,' Jane wrote to Cassandra. 'We found the roads in excellent order, had very good horses all the way. . .'.[5] From Bath she wrote to tell Cassandra of the latest fashions: 'Flowers are very much worn, & Fruit is still more the thing. – Eliz. has a bunch of Strawberries, & I have seen Grapes, Cherries, Plumbs & Apricots.'[6] But when she has to decide what to bring home, it seemed wiser – 'more natural' – to choose flowers for hat trimmings.

Two months after the Austens returned home from this first visit, they received news from Bath of an unfortunate drama involving the Leigh Perrots; it is an episode which remains puzzling.

One morning in August 1799 Mr and Mrs Leigh Perrot strolled out and called at a haberdasher's shop to buy a length of black lace. They paid for it and went on their way. Returning home they were accosted by the shop assistant who asked if the packet contained black *and white* lace. It was duly opened and found to contain both black and white. A mistake, of course, said Mrs Leigh Perrot, handing back the white lace, and she and her husband walked on home. That evening the owner of the shop went to the Guildhall and made a charge of attempted larceny. At that time, theft of any article valued at more than one shilling was punishable by death or transportation to Australia for seven years. Mrs Leigh Perrot was committed to Ilchester gaol to await trial at the next Assizes, due to be held in Taunton in March 1800. Mr Leigh Perrot accompanied his wife to Ilchester, where they were able to lodge in the gaoler's house.

Although she was not a favourite aunt there must nevertheless have been consternation at Steventon Rectory. In January Mrs Austen offered to send one or both her daughters to keep her sister-in-law company, but the offer was refused; the accused could not 'let those Elegant young Women be Inmates in a Prison'.[7] Nor would she allow them to support her at the trial: 'To have two Young Creatures gazed at in a public Court would cut one to the very heart.'[8] The trial lasted six hours, although the jury took only fifteen minutes to return a verdict of 'Not guilty'. There have been suggestions that Mrs Leigh Perrot was in fact an accomplished kleptomaniac and her accusers well known rogues who hoped to be bought off by the well-to-do couple.

When Mr and Mrs Austen, Cassandra and Jane moved to Bath in 1801 they left behind many good friends in Hampshire, but the Leigh Perrots had friends in the city and although their circle may have been somewhat staid, even dull, they would have been happy to chaperone two good-looking young women. Bath may have passed its heyday, but there were still balls and concerts on alternate evenings in the season. Balls began at 6 pm and ended at 11 pm; they were presided over by a Master of Ceremonies who found partners for newcomers and arranged the dances. After a ball in May 1801, Jane wrote to Cassandra: 'I dressed myself as well as I could, & had all my finery much admired at home. By nine o'clock my Uncle, Aunt & I entered the rooms & linked Miss Winstone on to us. – Before tea, it was rather a dull affair; but then the beforetea did not last long, for there was only one dance, danced by four couple. – Think of four couple, surrounded by about an hundred people, dancing in the upper rooms at Bath!'[9]

There is an echo of this in a letter from young

George Lefroy at Ashe Rectory. He was on vacation from Oxford and had gone to enjoy himself at one of the regular subscription dances in Basingstoke. 'Everybody seemed out of spirits and the few Gentlemen who were there were so lazy that they would not all dance, even tho' there were ladies sitting by.'[10]

Although life in Bath may have seemed to Jane dull and trivial, and as far as can be ascertained she did no writing during the four years she spent there, in fact she was acquiring excellent impressions and experiences to use in *Northanger Abbey* and *Persuasion*. Lying as it does in a hollow, Bath can be stuffy and enervating in summer; with open drains, and horses fouling the dusty roads and attracting swarms of flies, it must also have been intolerably smelly. So once the Austens had settled in, the four of them set off for a holiday in the West Country.

In 1803 the fragile Peace of Amiens was broken and France and England were once again at war. In Hampshire Mrs Lefroy was greatly perturbed about the possibility of a French invasion. In a letter to her second son Edward, who was studying at a tutor's establishment in the Isle of Wight, she warned him to be careful going out in the evening for fear of being caught by the press-gang out looking for able-bodied men to serve in naval ships.[11] In another letter she passes on her husband's instruction that if drilling for the Volunteers takes place on Sundays 'during the time of Divine Service he does not wish you to attend, but if it is only after Church he does not think there is any wrong in it.'[12]

In July 1803 Mrs Lefroy's letter to Edward gives him news of progress in organizing Volunteers in the Ashe, Deane and Steventon area – men of all sorts and conditions, who were to be given elementary training in preparation for the expected invasion. She relates how James Austen and George Lefroy have ridden round four parishes and collected one hundred names. Mr Holder of Ashe Park, who is to be the senior officer, has subscribed £50 and so has Mr Lefroy; the young ones have each contributed £10. Arms and uniforms have been requested from Lord Bolton, in command of the Hampshire Volunteers. James Austen and the Lefroys' son-in-law, the Revd Henry Rice, curate at Deane, may have been disgruntled when Lord Bolton decreed that clergymen should not hold military commissions. Altogether, 120 men were signed up but their attendance at drills must have been dependent on the demands of haymaking and harvest.

In January 1804 Mrs Lefroy wrote: 'Invasion is still the story in this neighbourhood but I do not believe it will take place until the spring.'[13] In May, when the captain, Mr Holder, was away, Ensign George Lefroy took a contingent to join a review of 500 Volunteers at Basingstoke. By November some weapons and uniforms must have arrived because the Ashe–Deane–Steventon contingent fired for the first time. In the following month, December 1804, Mrs Lefroy died following a fall from her horse on a frosty afternoon. It was in fact on Jane Austen's birthday. Four years later Jane expressed her deep feelings of grief in a long poem which begins:

> The day returns again, my natal day;
> What mix'd emotions with the Thought arise!
> Beloved friend, four years have pass'd away
> Since thou wert snatch'd forever from our eyes.

The language is stilted and formal. Jane's most remarkable achievement is the poem she wrote a few days before her death in July 1817. The poem relates to the power of St Swithin, the patron saint of Winchester, to bring rain in July to Winchester.

Jane's mother had a gift for writing verse and several of her family inherited this, though none were so skilful. The ability to find appropriate words to rhyme amused her and she could turn out a witty poem for any occasion. Her verses are lively and can be read today with pleasure. Of her sons, James was the most prolific versifier. Throughout his life he turned to poetry, sometimes for fun or to express deeper emotions. With their talent for writing and using words the family would enjoy evenings at home composing charades and riddles.

Now that their parents were comfortably settled in Bath, Cassandra and Jane were able to leave them and enjoy a round of visits to friends and family, including of course James and Mary at Steventon. They planned to stay for a couple of weeks with their good friends Catherine and Alethea Bigg at Manydown, a fine country house near Steventon where they had enjoyed many happy evenings in former years, at parties and dances. Now, during the course of an evening at Manydown, Catherine and Alethea's brother Harris Bigg Wither took the opportunity to propose to Jane – and was accepted. But during the night – surely a sleepless one – she changed her mind. At daybreak a carriage was ordered from the stables; Cassandra and Jane fled to Steventon, and despite the inconvenience to him, they insisted that James escort them to Bath immediately.

The Bigg sisters generously forgave Jane for rejecting their brother, and the friendship endured. Harris and Jane had known each other since childhood. Jane may have been tempted by the prospect of settling down in a fine house with a well-to-do husband. 'And though she was not a slave to worldly considerations she thought it a mistake to overlook them entirely. It was wrong to marry for money, but it was silly to marry without it.'[14]

A long time after, Caroline wrote down what her mother had told her of this incident:

Mr Wither was very plain in person – awkward, & even uncouth in manner – nothing but his size to recommend him – he was a fine big man – but one need not look about for secret reasons to account for a young lady's *not* loving him – a great many would have taken him without love. . . . He had sense in plenty & went through life very respectably, as a country gentleman – I *conjecture* that the advantages he could offer & her gratitude for his love, & her long friendship with his family, induced my Aunt to decide that she would marry him *when* he should ask her – but that having accepted him she found she was miserable & that the place and fortune which would certainly be *his,* could not alter the *man*.[15]

Harris picked himself up. In May 1804 Mrs Lefroy wrote to her son: 'Harris Wither is at home and in high spirits. Col. and Mrs Frith and their daughter [Anne] are expected at Manydown the beginning of next month.' And in September she mentioned 'Harris and his bride'.

F O U R

LYME REGIS

In November 1803 Mr and Mrs Austen and their daughters took a holiday in Lyme Regis, a sheltered small town in pretty wooded country on the borders of Dorset and Devon. It had fairly recently become known as a seaside watering-place, but was less fashionable than Brighton, Southampton or Weymouth; it was probably less expensive. Lyme Regis's colourful history would have interested George Austen. During the Civil War it was a parliamentary stronghold. The Royalist Prince Maurice brought an army of six thousand men to capture the town and its useful harbour for the king, but wisely withdrew when eight vessels arrived in the harbour with supplies of food and ammunition for the defenders. In 1685 the Duke of Monmouth landed on the beach at the start of his ill-fated expedition to claim the throne from James II. He managed to rally about two thousand men to his cause and set off north for Somerset, but his army was defeated at the Battle of Sedgemoor and the duke was executed. Twelve of his supporters were hanged at Lyme Regis.

Jane was captivated by the town and made it, in addition to Bath, the setting for *Persuasion*, the last novel she completed. This description shows what delighted her:

> The remarkable situation of the town, the principal street almost hurrying into the water, the walk to the Cobb, skirting round the pleasant little bay, which, in the season, is animated with bathing machines and company; the Cobb itself, its old wonders and new improvements, with the very beautiful line of cliffs stretching out to the east of the town, are what the stranger's eye will seek; and a very strange stranger it must be, who does not see charms in the immediate environs of Lyme, to make him wish to know it better.[1]

On this second visit to Lyme Regis the Austens brought the cook, Jenny, from Bath, as well as Molly the maid, but James, who waited at table, is thought to have been hired locally, because when they returned home he was most keen to go with them to Bath.

Lyme Regis boasted Assembly Rooms which though small included a ballroom, a billiard-room, and a card-room where copies of several daily and most of the county newspapers were to be found. It was supported by subscribers and open all year round. Tuesdays and Thursdays were Public Nights. During the season a ball was held on Tuesday evenings, with stewards to introduce partners and superintend the dancing. 'The music will be ready at eight o'clock. Tea in the ball-room for dancers after the first set.' Tea and coffee were supplied at 7 pm for card players. The music was usually supplied by three violins and a violincello.

On 14 September 1804 Jane wrote to Cassandra:

The Ball last night was pleasant, but not full for Thursday. My Father staid very contentedly till half-past nine – we went a little after eight – & then walked home with James & a Lanthorn, tho' I believe the Lanthorn was not lit, as the Moon was up. . . . My Mother & I staid about an hour later. Nobody asked me the first two dances – the two next I danced with Mr Crawford – & had I chosen to stay longer might have danced with Mr Granville, Mrs Granville's son – whom my dear friend Miss Armstrong offered to introduce to me – or with a new, odd looking Man who had been eyeing me for some time, & at last without any introduction asked me if I meant to dance again.[2]

Jane also tells her sister that she had called on Miss Armstrong in the morning and was introduced to her father and mother. 'Like other young Ladies she is considerably genteeler than her Parents; Mrs Armstrong sat darning a p^r of Stockings the whole of my visit. . . . We afterwards walked together for an hour on the Cobb; she is very conversable in a common way; I do not perceive Wit or Genius – but she has Sense & some degree of Taste, & her manners are very engaging.'[3] Jane's comment shows clearly the novelist's unceasing eye, the clues which showed Mrs Armstrong's lack of accepted behaviour towards visitors. Mrs Armstrong may have thought she knew Jane well enough to carry on darning – but clearly Jane didn't think so.

The Cobb at Lyme Regis was first constructed in medieval times to protect the harbour from the sea, but has been rebuilt many times. It has a wide promenade on top and, as Jane and Miss Armstrong found, is a most agreeable way to enjoy sea breezes. The Cobb provides the setting for the dramatic scene in *Persuasion*:

There was too much wind to make the high part of the new Cobb pleasant for the ladies, and they agreed to get down the steps to the lower, and all were contented to pass quietly and carefully down the steep flight, excepting Louisa; she must be jumped down them by Captain Wentworth. In all their walks he had had to jump her down from the stiles; the sensation was delightful to her. The hardness of the pavement for her feet made him less willing upon the present occasion; he did it however; she was safely down, and instantly, to show her enjoyment, ran up the steps to be jumped down again. He advised her against it, thought the jar too great; but no, he reasoned and talked in vain; she smiled and said, 'I am determined I will;' he put out his hands; she was too precipitate by half a second, she fell on the pavement on the Lower Cobb, and was taken up lifeless![4]

The steps described were rough blocks of stone projecting from the wall to form a way down to the Lower Cobb. While staying in Bridport in 1867 the poet Alfred Tennyson walked the nine miles over the hills to Lyme and, refusing all refreshment, said at once: 'Now take me to the Cobb, and show me the steps from which Louisa Musgrove fell.'[5] Many of today's visitors behave in a similar way.

During their stay in Lyme the Austens called on Mr Austen's former pupil, Richard Buller, and his wife. Buller was now the vicar of a parish on the coast not far from Lyme. Henry Austen and Eliza also took the opportunity to enjoy a holiday by the sea, and stayed for a while with the Austens.

Several weeks after returning to Bath, George Austen was taken ill. He died a few days later, on 21 January 1805. Henry was able to go immediately to Bath; Charles was far away on the Atlantic seaboard of America and only received the news much later. Jane wrote immediately to Frank – twice, in fact, for after sending her letter to him at Dungeness, she learned that his ship had sailed for Portsmouth. In the first letter she wrote: 'Our dear Father has closed his virtuous & happy life, in a death almost as free from suffering as his Children could have wished . . . – My Mother bears the Shock as well as possible; she was quite prepared for it, & feels all the blessing of his being spared a long Illness. . . . I wish I could have given you better preparation – but it has been impossible.'[6]

The funeral service was at Walcot Church, where

in 1764 George and Cassandra were married. Mrs Austen and her daughters were now left with a modest income, but her sons decided immediately to contribute what each could afford, in order to provide them with an assured income of £450 a year.

FIVE

SOUTHAMPTON

Mrs Austen and her daughters stayed in Bath but in March 1805 they moved into cheaper lodgings. In June they set off on a round of visits to relations in Kent and Hampshire. In March 1806 Mrs Austen returned to Bath in a vain search for an affordable home. She had already invited their good friend Martha Lloyd to live henceforth as one of the family, following the death of her mother. This was to have the advantage of enabling Cassandra and Jane to get away, leaving Mrs Austen in Martha's care.

While awaiting a sea-going appointment, Frank, by now a captain, had taken a lease on a large house in Castle Square, Southampton. Since the Royal Navy's bustling naval base at Portsmouth was not too distant, Frank was able to keep in touch with naval events and be on hand when needed. He suggested that Mrs Austen and her household should join him and his bride Mary – known to the family as 'Mrs F.A.', to distinguish her from the other Mary, James's wife, known as 'Mrs J.A.'. But before joining Frank and Mary, Mrs Austen decided to call on her cousin, the Revd Thomas Leigh, rector of Adlestrop in Gloucestershire. During their visit news came that he had inherited the ancestral Leigh property, Stoneleigh Abbey, a few miles away; it seemed politic to claim his inheritance without delay, and his cousin and her daughters accompanied him. Although she had often stayed at Edward's fine house in Kent, this was Jane's first experience of staying in a great aristocratic mansion, with twenty-six bed chambers in the new part of the house, and the whole surrounded by 4½ acres of garden. Mrs Austen wrote to her daughter-in-law, 'Mrs J.A.':

And here we all found ourselves on Tuesday . . . Eating Fish, venison & all manner of good things, at a late hour, in a Noble large Parlour hung round with family Pictures – every thing is very Grand & very fine & very Large – The House is larger than I could have supposed – we can *now* find our way about it. I mean the best part, as to the offices . . . Mr Leigh almost dispairs [*sic*] of ever finding his way about them – I have proposed his setting up *directing Posts* at the Angles – I expected to find everything about the place very fine & all that, but I had no idea of its being so beautiful, I had figured to myself long Avenues, dark rookeries & dismal Yew Trees, but here are no such melancholy things; The Avon runs near the house amidst Green Meadows, bounding [*sic*] by large and beautiful Woods, full of delightful Walks. . . .[1]

From Stoneleigh the Austens moved on to Staffordshire to spend a month with Mrs Austen's nephew, Edward Cooper, and his wife, at Hamstall Ridware Rectory. (Edward's sister Jane had shared Cassandra's and Jane's brief schooling with Mrs Cawley and later at the Abbey School, Reading.)

The house Frank had found in Southampton for the extended household was old-fashioned, but it had a large garden. It was situated under the old city wall, with easy access to the ramparts and from there a view of Southampton Water. When any of Mrs Austen's grandchildren came to stay a special treat was to watch Lady Lansdowne leaving the mock Gothic castle on the opposite side of the square, in a little carriage drawn by eight ponies controlled by boy postillions.

Southampton was a lively town, with a theatre, good shops, circulating libraries and Assembly Rooms. But the Austens had few friends there and amused themselves with parlour games, reading aloud, and supporting Frank's pregnant wife. When an acquaintance gave them an introduction, Jane and Frank duly called: 'They live in a handsome style and are rich, and she seemed to like to be rich, and we gave her to understand that we were far from being so; she will soon feel therefore that we are not worth her acquaintance,'[2] wrote Jane to Cassandra.

This was written shortly after the Austens had taken stock of their finances and assessed expenditure. They decided they could manage, provided the rent of the house was not increased. While not on active service Frank would have been on half-pay.

This seemingly tranquil life, with the added interest of the coming birth of Frank and Mary's first child, was sadly interrupted when news came from Cassandra at Godmersham that Edward's wife Elizabeth had died suddenly, two weeks after the birth of their eleventh child. Jane hastily sent mourning clothes to her sister and attended to her own and her mother's. Edward's two sons were given leave from Winchester College and, after a few days at Steventon, they took the coach to

Southampton, travelling by choice on the outside and sharing the coachman's great-coat. Jane told her sister: '*They behave extremely* well in every respect, showing quite as much feeling as one wishes to see, and on every occasion speaking of their father with the liveliest affection.'[3] She adds: 'While I write now, George is most industriously making and naming paper ships, at which he afterwards shoots with horse-chestnuts, brought from Steventon on purpose.' Jane kept them occupied during the few days they stayed – walking on the walls to watch the tides rising and falling, taking a boating party up the river to see a naval ship under construction, and in the evening playing games round the table: spillikins was always a special favourite. Then the boys were put on the coach to return to school.

Edward did not marry again. He cared for his family and managed the estates he had inherited – two fine houses and surrounding land: Godmersham Park in Kent, and Chawton House, near Alton, in Hampshire. He only lived at Chawton for a few months when Godmersham was being redecorated. 'The Great House', as Chawton was called in the family, is a large rambling building with many small rooms. Some parts date from the sixteenth century, with wings added later. The long drive rises to the pink brick porch and front entrance, lawns cover the slope behind and fall away to the south side. New trees have been planted to replace those blown down in recent gales. The Great House has its own special charm, but it is not difficult to see why the Knight family (Edward had to take the surname Knight in order to come into his inheritance) preferred the elegant and spacious Godmersham Park, its extensive garden bordered by the River Stour. In between tenancies Edward lent the house to his naval brothers when they were on shore leave.

The Revd George Austen, Jane's father.
(Photograph courtesy of Jane Austen
Memorial Trust)

Mrs Cassandra Austen, Jane's
mother. (Photograph courtesy of
Jane Austen Memorial Trust)

Jane Austen, drawn by her sister
Cassandra, 1801. (National
Portrait Gallery)

Cassandra Elizabeth Austen, Jane's
beloved sister. (Photograph courtesy of
Jane Austen Memorial Trust)

James Austen, Jane's eldest brother, possibly painted by Cassandra. (Photograph courtesy of Jane Austen Memorial Trust)

Henry Austen, Jane's favourite brother, after he was ordained. (Photograph courtesy of Jane Austen Memorial Trust)

Edward Austen as a young man. In 1812 he and his children took the name Knight. (Photograph courtesy of Jane Austen Memorial Trust)

Frank Austen, as a young naval officer. (Private collection; photograph courtesy of Jane Austen Memorial Trust)

Charles Austen, Jane's youngest brother. (Private collection; photograph courtesy of Jane Austen Memorial Trust)

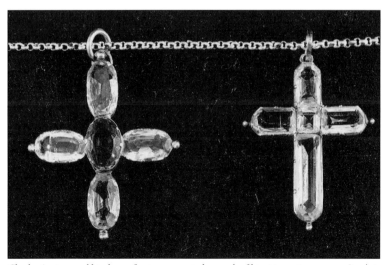

Charles Austen used his share of prize money to buy each of his sisters a topaz cross. Jane's is on the left, Cassandra's on the right. (Photograph courtesy of Jane Austen Memorial Trust)

Drawing of Steventon Rectory by Jane's niece, Anna Lefroy. (Photograph courtesy of Jane Austen Memorial Trust)

St Nicholas' Church, Steventon. (This drawing was kindly provided by Susan Woolley)

The Pump Room, Bath. Here, gentlemen would gather in the mornings to read the papers and discuss politics; the ladies would stroll up and down eyeing the new fashions, especially in bonnets. (The British Museum)

The house at Chawton as it is today. Mrs Austen, Jane, Cassandra and Martha Lloyd went to live there in 1809. (Photograph courtesy of Jane Austen Memorial Trust)

The house in College Street, Winchester, where Jane Austen died in July 1817.
(John Crook)

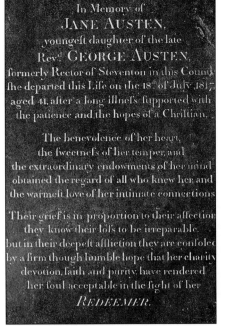

In Memory of
JANE AUSTEN,
youngest daughter of the late
Revᵈ GEORGE AUSTEN,
formerly Rector of Steventon in this County
she departed this Life on the 18ᵗʰ of July 1817,
aged 41, after a long illness supported with
the patience and the hopes of a Christian,

The benevolence of her heart,
the sweetness of her temper, and
the extraordinary endowments of her mind
obtained the regard of all who knew her, and
the warmest love of her intimate connections

Their grief is in proportion to their affection
they know their loss to be irreparable,
but in their deepest affliction they are consoled
by a firm though humble hope that her charity,
devotion, faith and purity, have rendered
her soul acceptable in the sight of her
REDEEMER.

Jane's tombstone in Winchester
Cathedral. (John Crook)

CHAWTON – THE EARLY YEARS

In 1808 Jane's brother Edward (Knight) offered his mother the choice of a house in Kent or a cottage on his Hampshire estate. She had little hesitation in choosing the cottage at Chawton, a small rural village within walking distance of the market town of Alton and riding distance of Steventon. The Austens were country people who had had to adjust to town life, with its visiting, evening parties in Bath and occasional balls in Southampton. Now aged 35 and 33, Cassandra and Jane no longer felt the need to keep up with changing fashions in dress. Except when concerned about her health their mother was a lively conversationalist, and good company. She was always interested in the smallest details of the lives of her large family circle. Now she was content to live in a modest house, leaving responsibility for the housekeeping to Cassandra while she took charge of the garden in order to provide fruit and vegetables for the household and for members of the family who called frequently at the cottage.

Although the rooms at Chawton were small, there was enough space for the four of them: Mrs Austen, Cassandra, Jane and Martha Lloyd. They kept a cook, a manservant, and a girl for the housework. Water had to be drawn from the well, bread was baked, and the laundry done at home.

Close by the house the main road divided, branching to Portsmouth on the left, and to Winchester and Southampton on the right. There would always have been the sound of horses, carriages and carts travelling in either direction.

James Austen's daughter Caroline went often as a child to see her grandmother and her aunts. She remembered 'a cheerful house – my Uncles, one or another, frequently coming for a few days; . . . the family talk had much of spirit and vivacity, and it was never troubled by disagreements as it was not their habit to argue with each other – There was always perfect harmony amongst the brothers and sisters.'[1]

For Mrs Austen, the cottage at Chawton 'fully

satisfied the moderate desires of one who had no taste for luxury or worldly state, and lived besides under the happy belief that what was decreed by those she loved must be wisest'.[2] There she lived contentedly for the rest of her life. A donkey carriage was purchased for her. Jane did her share in the work of running the house – her responsibility was to make the breakfast – and now, at last, she could settle down to writing, and had time to play her new piano, visit friends and family, and welcome her brothers and their wives and children.

In 1809 Jane wrote to Richard Crosby, the publisher who in 1803 had paid £10 for her manuscript of the novel then entitled 'Elinor and Marianne'. She asked about publication, saying that if the manuscript had been lost another copy could be supplied. The publisher replied that no date had been agreed for publication, and moreover the manuscript could be sent back if the sum paid six years earlier was returned. So Jane was able to recover the manuscript and change the title to *Sense and Sensibility*, and with help from her brother Henry, negotiate its publication by Thomas Egerton – her first published novel. It is believed she had revised it and rewritten some chapters. It is the story of three sisters and their widowed mother. Elinor, the eldest, is rational, controlled and capable. The second sister is a young, impetuous girl, with a hopeless passion for the cad Willoughby. Early in the story there is an example of Jane Austen's rare gift for dialogue when John Dashwood is discussing with his wife what help he should give to his mother and sisters who have just moved in to a small cottage close by. Each reveals his or her character without need of explanation.

In March 1811 Jane went to London, where she stayed with Henry and Eliza, at their elegant house in fashionable Sloane Street, to correct proofs of *Sense and Sensibility*. Henry's bank was prospering and he and Eliza enjoyed a full social life. Jane described one of their evening parties, to which eighty people had been invited:

There were many solicitudes, alarms & vexations beforehand of course, but at last everything was quite right. The rooms were dressed up with flowers &c, & looked very pretty. . . . At ½ past 7 arrived the Musicians in two Hackney coaches, & by 8 the lordly Company began to appear. . . . The Draw⁸ room being soon hotter than we liked, we placed ourselves in the connecting Passage, which was comparatively cool, & gave us all the advantage of the Music at a pleasant distance, as well as that of the first veiw [*sic*] of every new comer. – I was quite surrounded by acquaintance, especially Gentlemen; . . . The House was not clear till after 12.[3]

Jane enjoyed walking in London, dining out with Henry and Eliza and their friends, and evenings at the theatre, though she was much disappointed to miss seeing the great Mrs Siddons. Henry had been misinformed by the box-keeper about the dates of her appearance on stage when he went to buy tickets.

Jane returned home in May and as Cassandra was once again at Godmersham, it is from Jane's letters to her that one learns of friends and family coming to Chawton, and of the wilful niece Anna, who was staying at Chawton in Cassandra's absence. Because Cassandra could not make plans to return home until she had a male escort, in June Henry took his gig to Godmersham, spent a few days there, and then brought Cassandra to London; it is not known who escorted her back to Chawton.

Sense and Sensibility was published in the autumn in three volumes, price 15s, but it was not reviewed until the spring of 1812.

In April 1813 Jane was asked to come to London to help Henry during the last days of a painful illness suffered by Eliza. She went again, after Eliza's death, to help in clearing up her possessions before Henry moved from Sloane Street to premises above his bank's office in Covent Garden.

Encouraged by seeing her first novel in print, Jane now offered another manuscript to her publisher, Thomas Egerton. This was *Pride and Prejudice*, revised and probably rewritten in large part since Mr Austen had offered the manuscript, entitled 'First Impressions', to a publisher in 1797. A novel with that title had been published in 1800, which probably explains the new title. The words 'pride and prejudice' are taken from Fanny Burney's novel *Cecilia* (1782).

'I want to tell you that I have got my own darling Child from London,'[4] Jane wrote to Cassandra when she received the first author's copy of *Pride and Prejudice*. That same day a neighbour came to dine with Mrs Austen and Jane in Chawton. Mrs Austen read aloud the first part of the first volume, and the guest never suspected that the author was in the room. Jane commented to Cassandra: 'She really does seem to admire Elizabeth. I must confess that *I* think her as delightful a creature as ever appeared in print, & how I shall be able to tolerate those who do not like *her* at least, I do not know.'[5]

The following week Jane told Cassandra that she had been much depressed after the second evening's reading to the same neighbour, but thought this might be attributed to her Mother's too rapid reading. 'Upon the whole however I am quite vain enough & well satisfied enough. – The work is rather too light & bright & sparkling; – it wants shade.' She goes on to suggest that it would be improved by a long chapter about something unconnected with the story, anything that would 'bring the reader with increased delight to the playfulness . . . of the general stile [*sic*].'[6] Fortunately she never did this.

Reviews of the book appeared in literary journals in February and March 1813. The *British Critic*[7] said that *Pride and Prejudice* was 'far superior to almost all the publications of the kind which have come before us'. The *New Review*[8] also commented favourably: 'There is not one person in the drama with whom we could readily dispense.' That is surely the opinion still. We would not want to lose any of the characters – not even Mr Bingley's brother-in-law, 'who lived only to eat, drink, and play cards'.

There was, meanwhile, much speculation among the novel-reading aristocracy about the identity of the authoress – as the title page simply stated it was 'By the author of "Sense and Sensibility".'

In May 1813 Jane took advantage of Henry's visit to Chawton to travel to London with him. There he took her to an exhibition of paintings, and she amused herself by looking for representations of characters in *Pride and Prejudice*. She found Mrs Bingley, 'dressed in white with green ornaments', but could not find a picture of anyone resembling 'Mrs Darcy'. Nor could she discover her at an exhibition of 130 of Sir Joshua Reynolds' paintings. Jane was delighted to find herself being driven round London in a barouche, open in the summer weather.

Henry was so proud of his sister that he could not resist telling his friends the name of the author of the novel which was being much talked about. The secret was also revealed to the nephews and nieces. This prompted James's son Edward, a schoolboy of fifteen, to express his admiration in verse:

No words can express, my dear Aunt, my surprise
Or make you conceive how I opened my eyes,
Like a pig Butcher Pile has just struck with his knife,
When I heard for the very first time in my life
That I had the honour to have a relation
Whose works were dispersed through the whole of
    the nation.[9]

Encouraged by good reviews and the news that 'every copy of S. & S. is sold and that it has brought me £140', Jane began to think seriously about her next book. She wrote to Frank, then commanding HMS *Elephant* as part of the fleet patrolling the North Sea to prevent Napoleon making use of ports: 'I have something in hand — which I hope on the credit of P. & P. will sell well, tho' not half so entertaining. And by the bye — shall you object to my mentioning the Elephant in it, & two or three other of your old Ships? I *have* done it, but it shall not stay, to make you angry. — They are only just mentioned.'[10] Jane was at the time working on *Mansfield Park*.

During 1813 Jane and Henry went to stay at Godmersham, their brother Edward's house. One of his daughters, Marianne Knight, remembered later:

When Aunt Jane came to us at Godmersham she used to bring the MS of whatever novel she was writing with her, and would shut herself up with my elder sisters in one of the bedrooms to read them aloud. I and the younger ones used to hear peals of laughter through the door, and thought it very hard that we should be shut out from what was so delightful. I also remember how Aunt Jane would sit quietly working beside the fire in the library, saying nothing for a good while, and then would suddenly burst out laughing, jump up and run across the room to a table where pens and paper were lying, write something down, and then come back to the fire and go on quietly working as before.[11]

There was consternation at Chawton when in September 1813 James's daughter, the wayward Anna, announced her engagement to Ben, the youngest son of Jane's good friend Mrs Lefroy. He had a little money of his own but no profession or income. Jane told Frank:

It came upon us without much preparation; – at the same time, there was *that* about her which kept us in a constant preparation for something. – We are anxious to have it go on well, there being quite as much in his favour as the Chances are likely to give her in any Matrimonial connection. I beleive [*sic*] he is sensible, certainly very religious, well connected & with some Independance. There is an unfortunate dissimularity of Taste between them in one respect which gives us some apprehensions, he hates company & she is very fond of it; – This, with some queerness of Temper on his side & much unsteadiness on hers, is untoward.[12]

In the autumn of 1813 Jane was staying at Henry's house in London when Edward brought three of his younger children to stay in Covent Garden. Jane was kept busy taking the girls round London. She shared with Cassandra news from the dress- or corset-maker: 'to my high amusement, that the stays now are not made to force the Bosom up at all; – *that* was a very unbecoming, unnatural fashion.'[13]

She took Louisa, aged eight, and Marianne, twelve, to the dentist. Marianne had two teeth taken out in order to make room for those in the front: 'We heard each of the two sharp hasty Screams. . . . It was a disagreeable hour.'[14] The girls, were, however, enchanted by evenings at the theatre ('I speak of *them*; my delight was very tranquil'), especially when they saw *Don Juan*, a pantomime – '& I must say I have seen nobody on the stage who has been a more interesting Character than that compound of Cruelty & Lust.'[15]

When Edward took his girls home to Godmersham, Jane went too, possibly to give her leisure to finish the manuscript of *Mansfield Park*, and to start work on her next book, *Emma*, though, as she told Frank, 'In this House there is a constant succession of small events, somebody is always going or coming.'[16] She might have added 'with plenty of servants to look after them'. One expedition Jane undertook with Edward, a magistrate, was to Canterbury to inspect the gaol.

SEVEN

CHAWTON – THE
LATER YEARS

Towards the end of 1813, when *Mansfield Park* was completed, Henry Austen probably helped Jane to get it published. This time Thomas Egerton was less enthusiastic but he agreed to publish it on commission: Jane would receive royalties after the cost of printing and binding had been recovered from sales. In March 1814 she stayed with Henry in London to correct proofs. She told Cassandra: 'He says it is very different from the other two [*Sense and Sensibility* and *Pride and Prejudice*], but does not appear to think it at all inferior.'[1] While she was in London Jane had the opportunity to see the great Edmund Kean play Shylock in *The Merchant of Venice*.

Although it was not reviewed anywhere, *Mansfield Park* sold out during the year, bringing Jane a profit of £350. Perhaps to give herself reassurance, Jane collected comments from the family and from friends. Frank gave his opinion: 'We certainly do not think it as a *whole*, equal to P. & P. – but it has many & great beauties. Fanny is a delightful Character! and Aunt Norris is a great favourite of mine. The Characters are natural & well supported, & many of the Dialogues are excellent. – You need not fear the publication being considered as discreditable to the talents of its Author.'[2]

Mansfield Park is in many ways the most interesting and the most complex of all Jane Austen's novels. The heroine has been called a wimp, a prig, or a doughty champion of moral values. She is all these and much more. Her midshipman brother is a delightful reminder of the Austen brothers when young. The proposed amateur performance of *Lovers' Vows* by Kotzebue is based on plays staged at Steventon when the young Jane watched her brothers and their friends struggling with their lines. And Charles Austen's generous gift of a topaz cross and gold chain to each of his sisters also finds a place in the novel, before the ball Fanny's uncle gives in her honour. With her usual skill, Jane Austen makes sure that in the end Fanny is betrothed (though not everyone would agree that she was right to marry Edmund).

During the summer of 1814 there was much anxiety at Chawton. Mrs Austen, her daughters and Martha Lloyd might be evicted when Edward Knight was sued by residents in the village, hitherto good friends, for possession of much of his Chawton estate. It was a complicated legal tangle based on the terms of an ancient will and conditions attaching to the entail. Edward stood his ground but the lawsuit dragged on for four years and he had to pay his adversaries a large sum.

When Frank rented the Great House at Chawton from his brother, his large family would have been ten minutes' walk away from Mrs Austen and the aunts in the cottage. James would bring his daughter Caroline over from Steventon so that the young cousins could play together. Later, Caroline wrote her memories of these years:

> I did not *dislike* Aunt Cassandra — but if my visit had at any time chanced to fall out during *her* absence, I don't think I should have missed her — whereas, *not* to have found Aunt Jane at Chawton, *would* have been a blank indeed.
>
> Her charm to children was great sweetness of manner — she seemed to love you, and you loved her naturally in return. . . . When cousins came to share

the entertainment, she would tell us the most delightful stories chiefly of Fairyland, and her Fairies had all characters of their own — The tale was invented, I am sure, at the moment, and was sometimes continued for 2 or 3 days.[3]

In November 1814 Anna was married at Steventon to Ben Lefroy. James Austen gave his daughter away and Ben's eldest brother came from Ashe Rectory to read the marriage service. Mrs Austen was delighted when Ben and Anna returned to Hampshire the following year. They were able to rent part of Wyards, a large farmhouse within walking distance of Chawton.

During November Jane went to London to discuss with her publisher the possibility of a second edition of *Mansfield Park*. This Egerton refused to do. So when Jane's next manuscript was completed in 1815 it was offered to John Murray (the publisher made famous two years earlier, when the first cantos of Byron's *Childe Harold* were a literary triumph and the author became the idol of fashionable London). Murray's reader 'had nothing but good to say about *Emma*'. Murray offered Jane £450, with the copyright of *Mansfield Park* and *Sense and Sensibility* included. At this critical moment in the negotiations Henry became alarmingly ill. In a panic, Jane sent express letters summoning her brothers and Cassandra. Fortunately Henry began to improve, and only Cassandra and Jane remained in London to look after him. When Henry could once again take a hand in negotiations with Murray, it was agreed that the firm would publish *Emma* on commission and also do a small reprint of *Mansfield Park*.

During Henry's illness he was attended by a Dr Charles Haden, a former neighbour; one of the Prince Regent's doctors was also called in. The latter told Jane that the Prince (the future George IV) greatly admired her novels and had a set of them in each of his residences. When the Prince was told that Jane Austen was in London, the Revd James Stanier Clarke, librarian at Carlton House, the royal residence in the Mall, was instructed to call and invite her to see the Prince's library. A time was agreed and on 13 November 1815 Jane was shown round Carlton House, with its opulent velvet and satin hangings, flowered carpets, marble pillars, and crimson drawing-room. Mr Clarke told Jane that he had been charged to ask that if she had a novel forthcoming, she would dedicate it to the Prince.

Although not admirers of the Prince Regent, Henry and Cassandra both considered Mr Clarke's words to be a command, not a request. As publication of *Emma* was imminent, there was no time to lose. John Murray's help had to be invoked, and within a few days the three volumes of *Emma*, with a long formal dedication to His Royal Highness in the first volume, were on their way to Carlton House. This handsome set, bound in scarlet morocco and with the Prince of Wales's feathers blocked in gold at the top of each spine, is now in the library at Windsor Castle.

In a letter thanking Jane for the present of a copy of each of her published novels, Mr Clarke suggested that she should 'delineate in some future Work the Habits of Life and Character and enthusiasm of a Clergyman – who should pass his time between the metropolis & the Country . . . Fond of, & entirely engaged in Literature – no man's Enemy but his own.'[4] Jane replied that although she might manage the comic part of the character, she could not possibly manage the literary. Indeed, a classical education, or at least an acquaintance with English literature, ancient and modern, would be essential. She added: 'I think

I may boast myself to be, with all possible Vanity, the most unlearned, & uninformed Female who ever dared to be an Authoress.'[5]

Mr Clarke was not easily deterred. He wrote again: 'Do let us have an English Clergyman after *your* fancy – much novelty may be introduced – shew dear Madam what good would be done if Tythes were taken away entirely, and describe him burying his own mother – as I did.'[6]

A few months later the importunate Mr Clarke bobbed up again, this time to suggest that Jane should dedicate her next novel to Prince Leopold of Coburg, who was to marry the Prince Regent's daughter Charlotte. Clarke, who had been appointed the Prince's chaplain and private English secretary, said: 'Any Historical Romance illustrative of the history of the august house of Cobourg, would just now be very interesting.'[7] 'No,' Jane replied, ' – I must keep to my own style & go on in my own Way; And though I may never succeed again in that, I am convinced that I should totally fail in any other.'[8]

EIGHT

THE LAST YEARS

In 1816 Jane began to feel increasingly unwell. With Cassandra she went to Cheltenham in the hope that the waters there – advertised as 'singularly efficacious in all bilious complaints, obstructions of the liver and spleen' – would cure her. It is now believed that she was in fact suffering from Addison's disease, a tubercular infection of glands beside the kidneys, a condition not diagnosed for another forty years. Modern drugs would have helped, but not spa water.

Home once more, she could sometimes manage the 1½-mile walk to Alton, though not the return. Thus encouraged, in January 1817 Jane began work on *Sanditon*, but after writing only eighty pages, she abandoned the lively and entertaining manuscript; it remained unfinished at her death.

At about this time Mrs Austen's brother, James Leigh Perrot, died. As he was wealthy and childless, Mrs Austen not unreasonably hoped to be remembered in his will, for she was almost totally dependent on the generosity and goodwill of her sons. However, so devoted was Mr Leigh Perrot to his wife that he left all his property to her. Not until after her death in 1836 did the surviving Austen sons and Cassandra each receive £1,000. The disappointment of Uncle James's will upset the already frail Jane severely.

Realizing that there was little hope of recovering her health, Jane made her own will: £50 was to go to Henry, and £50 to the French maidservant whom Eliza had long ago brought from France; everything else was to go to her 'dearest sister Cassandra'.

After she was particularly ill in May 1817, it was decided that Jane should go to Winchester to be in the care of a celebrated doctor at the County Hospital. James brought his carriage to Chawton and accompanied by Cassandra and Martha Lloyd, with Henry and a nephew riding on horseback in the rain beside the carriage, Jane was taken to lodgings in College Street, within sound of the cathedral's great bells. Gradually her strength failed, for Mr Lyford from the hospital could do nothing to help.

While still able to understand and share in the

responses, she received Holy Communion from James and Henry. At dawn on 18 July 1817 she died peacefully; she was buried in the north aisle of the cathedral.

Throughout her life Jane Austen had been guided by Christian principles, and she accepted the Church's teaching without question. Her faith is implicit in all her writing: the virtues of a disciplined life, a caring relationship between husband and wife, and their duty to give children a moral and loving upbringing, are reflected in her letters and in her novels. At her death she expected to appear before God and be judged.

Cassandra wrote to Fanny Knight: 'I *have* lost a treasure, such a Sister, such a friend as never can have been surpassed, – She was the sun of my life, the gilder of every pleasure, the soother of every sorrow, I had not a thought concealed from her, & it is as if I had lost a part of myself.'[1] '"Aunt Jane" was the delight of all her nephews and nieces,' her nephew wrote many years later. 'We did not think of her as being clever, still less as being famous; but we valued her as one always kind, sympathising, and amusing.'[2]

After the funeral, 'her brothers [Edward, Henry

and Frank] went back sorrowing to their several homes. They were very fond and very proud of her. They were attached to her by her talents, her virtues, and her engaging manners; and each loved afterwards to fancy a resemblance in some niece or daughter of his own to the dear sister Jane, whose perfect equal they never expected to see.'[3]

Mrs Austen continued to be cared for at Chawton by Cassandra and Martha Lloyd, and despite a constant preoccupation with her ailments, she lived to the age of eighty-seven. 'I almost think sometimes that God Almighty has forgotten me; but I daresay He will come for me in His own good time,' she once said to her grandson Edward. She died in 1827, ten years after Jane.[4]

NINE

AUNT JANE AND HER NIECES AND NEPHEWS

Among her large collection of nieces and nephews Jane had three special favourites: Fanny Knight, Anna Lefroy and Edward Austen-Leigh.

Fanny was the eldest of Edward's motherless children, and the same age as Anna. The Knight children were all brought up at Godmersham, the boys going away to school, and the girls having a succession of governesses. As Fanny was fifteen when her mother died, she not only had to be a mother to the younger children but also had to run the household for her father, acting as hostess to the aunts, uncles and friends who turned up to stay at Godmersham. Fanny kept a diary – sixty-nine notebooks survive – and it is from this, together with Jane's letters, that we know so much about their affectionate friendship.

Jane wrote to Cassandra: 'I am greatly pleased with your account of Fanny; I found her in the summer just what you describe, almost another Sister, & could not have supposed that a neice [*sic*] would ever have been so much to me. She is quite after one's own heart; give her my best Love, & tell her that I always think of her with pleasure.'[1]

In 1809, when her cousin Anna came to stay for several months, Fanny learned of the joys and hazards of falling in love, for Anna was considering an engagement not approved by her father. But before long it was Fanny who was in need of advice and without a mother who better than Aunt Jane to help her choose from a bewildering collection of young men? In 1814, in great confusion about her admirers, Fanny turned to Aunt Jane for counsel and was not disappointed. Fanny fancied herself in love with 'Mr J.P.'. 'Oh! dear Fanny,' Jane wrote:

Your mistake has been one that thousands of women fall into. He was the *first* young Man who attached himself to you. That was the charm, & most powerful it is . . . what is to be done? You certainly *have* encouraged him to such a point as to make him feel almost secure of you. . . . And now, my dear Fanny, having written so much on one side of the question, I shall turn round & entreat you not to commit yourself farther, & not to think of accepting him unless you really do like him. Anything is to be preferred or endured rather than marrying without Affection.[2]

Jane wrote again to Fanny concerning Mr J.P.: 'You frighten me out of my Wits by your reference. Your affection gives me the highest pleasure, but indeed you must not let anything depend on my opinion. Your own feelings & none but your own, should determine such an important point.'[3]

By 1817 Fanny was being wooed by a most suitable neighbour from Chilham Castle, an estate on the boundary of Godmersham. Jane wrote:

I have pretty well done with Mr Wildman. By your description he can*not* be in love with you, however he may try at it, & I could not wish the match unless there were a great deal of Love on his side. . . . Well, I shall say, as I have often said before, Do not be in a hurry; depend upon it, the right Man will come at

79

last; you will in the course of the next two or three years, meet with somebody more generally unexceptionable than anyone you have yet known, who will love you as warmly as ever *He* did, & who will so completely attach you, that you will feel you never loved before.[4]

There was no Aunt Jane to turn to when Fanny did become engaged at the age of twenty-seven. Sir Edward Knatchbull, Bt, a widower with five children, the eldest aged thirteen, was twelve years older than Fanny. Their marriage added nine children to the family circle.

Fanny has not been forgiven for a note she wrote in 1869, when Edward Austen-Leigh was collecting information from those who remembered Aunt Jane. In it she claimed that Cassandra and Jane were not as *refined* as they ought to have been, but that Aunt Jane was clever enough to put aside 'all possible signs of "common-ness"'.[5] However, Fanny was writing when Victorian rules of respectability prevailed. Her husband had been a Member of Parliament for many years, and for a short time in the Cabinet. Nevertheless, there are many who find Fanny's sharp comments about Jane and Cassandra a sad betrayal. After his wife's death James educated

Anna himself and he did it well. However, she was not taught the ladylike accomplishments of music, dancing and singing, and she became known as the prettiest but the worst-dressed girl in the neighbourhood.

When James married Mary Lloyd he gave all his affection to his second wife's children, James Edward and Caroline. Although the pock-marked Mary was clever, cheerful and hospitable, her manner was often abrupt and sharp, and she had a tartness of temper from which even her own children suffered. She slighted Anna, making her feel unloved and unwanted. Fortunately Anna could always count on the constant love and affection of her grandmother and the two aunts who had cared for her when her own mother died.

In July 1814 Anna began to write a novel, which she called 'Which is the Heroine?'. She sent chapters to Aunt Jane for advice. These would be read aloud at Chawton and returned a few days later with comments. Writing about lords and ladies has pitfalls, advises Aunt Jane, for Anna does not really know how they talk or address one another. She must get her facts right: 'Twice you have put Dorsetshire for Devonshire. I have altered it.'[6] Two letters of September 1814 show that Jane treated Anna's work seriously, writing to her as an equal. As the manuscript no longer exists, it is not easy to assess fully Jane Austen's comments, but they give a glimpse of her creative mind, and the limits she set for herself. 'You are now collecting your People delightfully, getting them exactly into such a spot as is the delight of my life; — 3 or 4 Families in a Country Village is the very thing to work on — & I hope you will write a great deal more, & make full use of them while they are so very favourably arranged.'[7] '"A vortex of Dissipation", . . . it is such thorough novel slang — and so old, that I dare say Adam met with it in the first novel he opened.'[8]

Anna married Ben Lefroy and when she was expecting their second child her husband reluctantly agreed to be ordained. They made their home at Compton, near Guildford, where Ben was curate. Later Anna wrote that these were the happiest years of her life. When Ben's brother, the rector of Ashe, died, the benefice bought long ago for three generations became available, so Ben and Anna moved back to that pleasant rectory in Hampshire. Ben died six years later, leaving Anna a widow with a son and five daughters, their ages ranging from two to fourteen. Ben's elder brother gave the family a home for a while. Anna tried to complete Aunt Jane's unfinished manuscript, *Sanditon*, but abandoned it after a few chapters. She published two books for children, but they are dull reading, and show no trace of her earlier liveliness – or of Aunt Jane's genius.

Jane had a special affection for (James) Edward Austen-Leigh, her brother James's son by his second wife. He was not only good-looking but also had a sweet, affectionate nature. While he was at Winchester College Edward tried his hand at writing a novel, as his half-sister Anna was doing. Jane told her sister: 'Edward is writing a Novel – we have all heard what he has written – it is extremely clever; written with great ease & spirit; – if he can carry it on in the same way, it will be a firstrate work, & in a style, I think, to be popular. Pray tell Mary [Edward's mother] how much I admire it.'[9]

In the next surviving letter to Edward Jane writes the famous comment on her own work, with its deprecating acceptance of the self-imposed limits of her writing:

By the bye, my dear Edward, I am quite concerned for the loss your Mother mentions in her Letter; two Chapters & a half to be missing is monstrous! It is well that *I* have not been at Steventon lately, & therefore cannot be suspected of purloining them; . . . What should I do with your strong, manly, spirited Sketches, full of Variety & Glow? How could I possibly join them on to the little bit (two Inches wide) of Ivory on which I work with so fine a Brush, as produces little effect after much labour?[10]

(The 'little bit of Ivory' is a reference to the memo tablets carried by ladies in a reticule, or hung from the waist with ribbons: there is an example at Jane Austen's House, Chawton.)

Edward went to Oxford, took his degree and was ordained. He married pretty Emma Smith. His great-aunt Mrs Leigh Perrot approved of his choice and on her death in 1836 he became the owner of Scarlets, but the expense of living there obliged him to sell the house. It has since been demolished. Edward assumed the surname Leigh in 1837 when he inherited Scarlets from his aunt, Mrs Leigh Perrot.

In the mid-nineteenth century increasing

curiosity and interest in Jane Austen prompted Edward to collect from surviving members of the family their reminiscences of Aunt Jane. These he put together and published as *A Memoir of Jane Austen* in 1870.

TEN

WHY DID JANE AUSTEN NOT MARRY?

Women have a dreadful propensity for being poor — which is one very strong argument in favour of Matrimony.[1]

Why did Jane Austen, a lively and popular young woman, never settle down with a husband? Among the gentry, the level of society into which she was born, single women were without status. As a parson's daughter with no hope of a dowry, she knew that however attractive she may have been to the opposite sex, she had only a slender chance of finding a husband in the fairly restricted circle of acquaintances in Hampshire. Yet Cassandra, equally without money or property, fell in love and became engaged to Tom Fowle, one of her father's former pupils.

In *Pride and Prejudice* the business of Mrs Bennet's life was to get her five daughters married, for on the death of her husband the family's house would devolve by entail on to a cousin and she and the girls would be homeless. Did Mrs Austen ever wonder what was to become of her two girls? Or did she as a devout Christian believe that God would provide, or at least take care of them? She would assuredly have seen to it that Cassandra and Jane were well turned out for evening parties and Assembly Room balls, and for the grander evenings to which they were invited once a year by titled aristocrats living within driving distance of Steventon: Lord and Lady Bolton at Hackwood, Lord and Lady Dorchester at Kempshot, and the Earl of Portsmouth at Hurstbourne Park.

Again in *Pride and Prejudice*, the homely and plain Charlotte Lucas, the eldest in the family, faces up to her decision to marry the ludicrous Mr Collins:

> Her reflections were in general satisfactory. Mr Collins, to be sure, was neither sensible nor agreeable; his society was irksome, and his attachment to her must be imaginary. But still he would be her husband. Without thinking highly either of men or of matrimony, marriage had always been

her object; it was the only honourable provision for well-educated young women of small fortune, and, however uncertain of giving happiness, must be their pleasantest preservative from want. This preservative she had now obtained; and at the age of twenty-seven, without ever having been handsome, she felt all the good luck of it.[2]

As she explains to Elizabeth Bennet, 'I am not romantic, you know. I never was. I ask only a comfortable home; and considering Mr Collins's character, connections, and situation in life, I am convinced that my chance of happiness with him is as fair as most people can boast on entering the marriage state.'[3]

A perceptive reading of Jane Austen's letters shows that she was always on the look-out for a husband, assessing each young man who came her way. As she had a gift for sharp comments on the people she met, it is not always easy to distinguish between protective irony and genuine attraction. In one letter to Cassandra, Jane wrote from Kent: 'We went by Bifrons, & I contemplated with a melancholy pleasure, the abode of Him, on whom I once fondly doated.'[4] Bifrons was a fine Georgian house, the home of the parents of Edward Taylor, whom she would have met while staying at Godmersham with her brother Edward and his wife Elizabeth.

Another young man she came to know in Kent was Edward Bridges, the brother of her sister-in-law Elizabeth. He is believed to have proposed and been turned down by Jane. Jane Austen's own family of handsome and lively brothers would certainly have set a standard by which any potential husband would be measured.

It has been asserted that although Tom Lefroy was attracted to her, he jilted Jane, a parson's daughter with no prospect of a dowry. They flirted, enjoyed meeting at different parties over Christmas and New Year 1796, and may indeed have felt the strength of sexual attraction. As Jane implies in a letter to Cassandra, their interest in each other was noticed and remarked on. But when Tom came to Hampshire he was in no position to get entangled with Jane, nor with anyone else. He had only recently completed with distinction a degree course at the University of Dublin, and was about to begin three years of serious law studies in London. His father, who was a colonel in the British army, stationed in Ireland throughout his career, had sold his commission and settled in County Limerick.

Tom was the eldest of eleven children. While he was at university his useful but interfering bachelor great-uncle Benjamin Langlois had written to the Colonel: 'Thomas has everything in his temper and character that can conciliate affection. A good heart, a good mind, good sense, and as little to correct in him as ever I saw in one of his age.'[5]

In 1797 Tom went back to Ireland to be called to the Irish Bar; he took the opportunity to become engaged to Mary Paul, the only sister of his great friend from university days. Tom had come to know Mary during holidays from the university at the Paul estate in County Wexford.

Tom and Mary lived in Leeson Street, Dublin, where their nine surviving children were born and brought up. Tom was frequently away on circuit, first as a young barrister, and later as a judge. He represented Dublin University in Parliament at Westminster for eleven years.

Jane would never have been happy in Ireland, away from her parents and her beloved sister and brothers. She had a strong religious faith, but would she have wanted a sermon by every post, such as Tom wrote to his wife? In his old age Tom is reported to have said that he had been in love with

Jane Austen, but it was a boy's love. Jane was right to forget him.

Two years after Tom left Hampshire the Lefroys had another guest to stay: the Reverend Samuel Blackall. As a Fellow of his Cambridge college he was obliged to remain celibate, but he hoped in time to acquire a valuable college living in Somerset. He told Mrs Lefroy: 'It would give me particular pleasure to have an opportunity of improving my acquaintance with that family [the Austens] – with a hope of creating to myself a nearer interest. But at present I cannot indulge any expectation of it.'[6] Jane wrote to Cassandra: 'It is therefore most probable that our indifference will soon be mutual, unless his regard, which appeared to spring from knowing nothing of me at first, is best supported by never seeing me.'[7] It was not until 1812, when the benefice became vacant, that Blackall could get married.

During the Austens' years in Bath there are no mentions of possible admirers in the Pump Room or the Assembly Rooms, probably because the company tended to be older. However, during a round of visits to Hampshire in 1802, Jane did accept a proposal of marriage from Harris Bigg

Wither at Manydown, but during the night she changed her mind. He was six years younger than Jane, and if she was attracted by the prospect of returning to Hampshire as mistress of Manydown she would have had to wait until 1813, when Harris's father died and the property became his.

In the *Memoir* of his Aunt Jane, Edward Austen-Leigh wrote that Cassandra, many years after her sister's death, had said:

> While staying at some seaside place, they [the Austens] became acquainted with a gentleman, whose charm of person, mind and manners was such that Cassandra thought him worthy to possess and likely to win her sister's love. When they parted, he expressed his intention of soon seeing them again; and Cassandra felt no doubt as to his motives. But they never again met. Within a short time they heard of his sudden death. I believe that, if Jane ever loved, it was this unnamed gentleman: but the acquaintance had been short, and I am unable to say whether her feelings were of such a nature as to affect her happiness.[8]

In *Persuasion*, the last completed novel, which is written with a rare understanding of the constancy of the human heart, and of true enduring love, Anne Elliot is given a second chance. As a young girl of nineteen she had loved and been loved by Wentworth, an impecunious naval officer. Unwisely she heeded the advice of her godmother and ended the engagement. Wentworth went off to sea, was promoted and, through various successful naval engagements and the capture of enemy vessels, acquired a handsome fortune. Six years later Anne and Captain Wentworth met again, at Bath and at Lyme Regis. Finally he is able to say: 'I must learn to be happier than I deserve.' And Anne 'gloried in being a sailor's wife'.

Jane Austen was well aware that her brothers enjoyed a freedom she would never have. Their professions provided an income, and even when Henry lost his money as a banker an alternative career opened up. Cassandra and Jane had always to find a willing father or brother to accompany them when either wanted to travel by stage-coach. Jane saw that far too many women were burdened with child-bearing, and lost their health, their looks and sometimes their lives.

At what point did she decide that writing was far more important to her than the security of a home and the companionship of a man she could like but not love? It was not until Jane was thirty-six and her first book had been published – *Sense and Sensibility* – that she had real confidence in her skill as a novelist. With Cassandra's never-failing support and a strong family loyalty, she could at last have the security of a settled home at Chawton, even if Mrs Austen should not survive. It was there that she was able to write her novels.

ELEVEN

AFTER JANE'S DEATH

Although James had called on Jane frequently during her last months in Winchester, he did not feel well enough to cope with the emotional stress of the funeral, at which his son James Edward represented him. James's own health deteriorated and he died at Steventon two years later. The benefice of Steventon was owned by Edward Knight, who offered it immediately to Henry Austen for a term of four years, after which time his own fourth son, William Knight, would be old enough for ordination.

Now that he had a settled home, if only for a few years, Henry married again. He was wholly dependent on his earnings and on leaving Steventon became Master of Farnham Grammar School, with a modest extra stipend as curate at the parish church. In 1824 he was appointed perpetual curate at Bentley, a small village between Farnham and Alton, and remained there until 1839.

Frank's wife Mary died following the birth of their eleventh child. In time he married again, choosing an old friend of the family, Martha Lloyd, now sixty-three, who was still sharing the cottage at Chawton with Cassandra. Old Aunt Leigh Perrot was not pleased and changed her mind about leaving her beloved house Scarlets to the distinguished admiral. Instead, Frank received £10,000, which enabled him to buy a house near Portsmouth. He was promoted to Admiral of the Fleet and died in 1863 at the age of ninety-one – the last of Jane Austen's brothers.

After his wife died Charles Austen was appointed to run the coastguard service on a stretch of the Cornish coast, looking out for ships trying to smuggle goods. He married his sister-in-law, Harriet, who had taken charge of the children after Fanny's death. His naval career was not over. He was given command of a frigate based in Jamaica and was involved in the suppression of the slave trade in the West Indies, and then was once again actively engaged in the Mediterranean. By now aged seventy and a Rear Admiral, he was appointed Commander-in-Chief of the East India and China Station, but he died of cholera in Burma in 1852. He had 'won the hearts of all by his gentleness and kindness while he was struggling with disease'.[1]

In 1832 an enterprising publisher bought the copyright of Jane Austen's novels and included them in a series of 'Standard Novels'.

As for Steventon Church, it has stood on the hill for eight centuries, overlooking the village in the valley below. In springtime primroses and bluebells are in flower, and birds nest in the hedgerows of the wooded lane where long ago the Revd George and Mrs Austen, their sons and two daughters scurried up the hill from the rectory for Sunday morning and evening services, to the sound of the church's medieval bells – bells which still ring out over woods and fields in this quiet corner of Hampshire.

The cottage at Chawton remained in the Knight estate until after the Second World War; following an appeal for funds by the recently inaugurated Jane Austen Society, it was bought by Mr T. Edward Carpenter, as a memorial to his son who had been killed in the war. Tenants were rehoused and a Memorial Trust was established to administer Jane Austen's House as a museum. It exhibits a fine collection of memorabilia, books and furniture, and is open to the public daily, though only at weekends during January and February.

The Great House in Chawton is being renovated to house the Centre for the Study of Early English Women's Writing. The grounds are being restored to the landscape known to Edward Knight and Jane Austen.

JANE AUSTEN'S WORKS

1811 *Sense and Sensibility* Published in three volumes, with 'By a Lady' on the title page. It was first written about 1795 in the form of letters and read to the family. It was favourably reviewed and sold out. Its second edition was published in 1813 on commission – Jane Austen only received a royalty payment for copies sold after the cost of printing and binding had been paid. She earned £140 for the first edition and £20 for the second.

1813 *Pride and Prejudice* Written between October 1796 and August 1797. Her father wrote to a London publisher offering to send the manuscript of a novel, but the offer was declined by return of post. The manuscript was kept carefully by Jane Austen and revised in 1812, when its original title, 'First Impressions' was changed. The copyright was sold to a publisher for £110. The second edition was published in 1813, and the third, in two volumes, in 1817.

The title-page merely stated 'By the author of "Sense and Sensibility".' Both novels began to be discussed and recommended between friends, and there was speculation about the identity of the author.

1814   *Mansfield Park*   Begun in 1811 and completed in 1813. It was published in three volumes on commission in a small edition which quickly sold out, but the publisher declined to issue a second edition. Jane Austen may have earned £320. She offered the text to another publisher, John Murray, and herself paid the cost of printing and binding. John Murray kept 10 per cent from sales.

1816   *Emma*   Begun 21 January 1814, finished 29 March 1815. Published in three volumes, with a dedication to the Prince Regent, a great admirer of Jane's work, added just as the book was about to be printed.

Jane Austen would have earned from it a total of £372 12s 11d, before the deduction of losses on the second edition of *Mansfield Park*.

1818   *Northanger Abbey* and *Persuasion*   *Northanger Abbey* was probably written in 1798–9, and was entitled 'Susan'. In 1803 Jane Austen sold the manuscript to a publisher for £10, but it was not issued. In 1809 Jane Austen wrote to enquire if the manuscript had been lost, and offered to send a copy. She went on to say that if the publisher did not then issue the book she would feel at liberty to take it elsewhere. The reply came that no date had been agreed for publication.

In 1816, after the publication of *Emma*, Henry Austen bought back the manuscript of *Northanger Abbey* ('Susan') for £10, and had the satisfaction of pointing out to the publisher that the work 'so lightly esteemed' was by the author of *Pride and Prejudice*.

Persuasion was begun on 8 August 1815 and completed in 1816. The two novels were published posthumously by John Murray in four volumes, still with no name on the title page, but simply 'By the author of "Pride and Prejudice", "Mansfield Park", &c.' The volume also included a 'Biographical Notice'. By December 1818 Cassandra, who had inherited the rights 'of the author' to Jane Austen's work, was owed £479 1*s* 2*d*, plus a further £39 2*s* 6*d* when the remaining copies were sold.

After Jane Austen's death her novels were not reissued or available in print until 1833, when an enterprising publisher, Richard Bentley, added them to a series of 'Standard Novels'. Cassandra and Henry Austen were offered £250 each for the copyright of five novels; £40 was paid to the executor of the publisher of *Pride and Prejudice*.

Different Bentley editions continued to be available throughout the nineteenth century, but in single volumes once copyright had expired. Towards the end of the century illustrated editions were published with line-drawings by Hugh Thomson, or coloured plates by H.M. and C.E. Brock.

In the twentieth century the novels have never been out of print, either in cased or paperback editions. In 1923 R.W. Chapman edited the novels, which were published in five volumes, with a sixth containing the Minor Works.

In America *Emma* was the first to be published, in Philadelphia in 1816, though it is unlikely that this was known to Jane Austen. The other novels followed in 1832–3.

Minor Works

Following increasing interest in Jane Austen and her novels, in 1870 James Edward Austen-Leigh published *A Memoir of Jane Austen*. The following year a second edition appeared, to which was added 'Lady Susan', and fragments of two other unfinished tales. This was the first publication of *Lady Susan, The Watsons*, two cancelled chapters of *Persuasion*, and extracts from the uncompleted *Sanditon*, of which the whole text was not published until 1925.

Jane collected her early stories – Juvenilia – into three notebooks, labelled Volume the First, Volume the Second and Volume the Third. *Volume the First* was published in 1933 and *Volume the Second* in 1922, with the title *Love and Freindship* (*sic*). It included 'The History of England', with Cassandra's watercolour illustrations. *Volume the Third* was published in 1951 and contained the story 'Catharine, or The Bower' and the incomplete 'Evelyn'.

Letters of Jane Austen, edited with an introduction and critical remarks by Edward, Lord Brabourne (son of Jane Austen's niece Fanny Knight), was published in 1884. It was a selection in two volumes of Jane Austen's letters to her sister and to other members of the family.

In 1932 *Jane Austen's Letters to her Sister Cassandra and Others*, collected and edited by R.W. Chapman, was published. A second edition was issued in 1952. In 1995 a third edition, edited by Deirdre Le Faye, was published. This contains one or two additional items, re-dates some letters, and includes notes and indexes.

There have been many dramatizations for the stage, TV and films.

BIBLIOGRAPHY

Austen, Caroline *My Aunt Jane Austen*, Alton, Jane Austen Society, 1952, 1991

Austen-Leigh, J.E. *A Memoir of Jane Austen*, London, R. Bentley, 1870, 1871

Austen-Leigh, R.A. *Austen Papers 1704–1856*, London, Spottiswoode, Ballantyne, 1942

Cecil, David *A Portrait of Jane Austen*, London, Penguin, 1996

Collins, Irene *Jane Austen and the Clergy*, London, Hambledon, 1994

Gilson, David *A Bibliography of Jane Austen*, Oxford University Press, 1982; Winchester, St Paul's Bibliographies, 1997

Hill, Constance *Jane Austen, Her Homes and Her Friends*, London, John Lane, 1902

Honan, Park *Jane Austen: Her Life*, London, Weidenfeld & Nicolson, 1987, 1997

Jenkins, Elizabeth *Jane Austen: A Biography*, London, Gollancz, 1938; Indigo, 1996

Le Faye, Deirdre *Jane Austen: A Family Record*, London, British Library, 1989 (revised edition of *Life and Letters of Jane Austen*, by W. and R.A. Austen-Leigh, London, Smith & Elder, 1913)

— 'Anna Lefroy's Original Memories of Jane Austen', *Review of English Literature*, NS, xxxix, August 1988

— (coll. and ed.) *Jane Austen's Letters*, 3rd edn, Oxford, Oxford University Press, 1995

Bibliography

Nokes, David *Jane Austen*, London, Fourth Estate, September, 1997

Selwyn, David (ed.) *Jane Austen: Collected Poems and Verse of the Austen Family*, Manchester, Carcanet Press, in association with Jane Austen Society, 1996

Tomalin, Claire *A Biography of Jane Austen*, London, Viking Press, September, 1997

Tucker, George H. *A Goodly Heritage: a History of Jane Austen's Family*, Manchester, Carcanet New Press, 1983; to be reissued by Sutton Publishing as *A History of Jane Austen's Family*, 1998

I am much indebted to David Gilson's incomparable *Bibliography of Jane Austen* (Oxford: Clarendon Press, 1982; St Paul's Bibliographies, 1997), and to Deirdre Le Faye for an authoritative account of the Austen family in *Jane Austen: A Family Record* (British Library, 1989), the revised and enlarged version of *Jane Austen, her life and letters, a family record* by W. and R.A. Austen-Leigh (1913).

NOTES

CHAPTER ONE

1. Deirdre Le Faye, 'Anna Lefroy's Original Memories of Jane Austen', *Review of English Literature*, xxxix, August 1988, no. 155.
2. J.E. Austen-Leigh, *A Memoir of Jane Austen* (Richard Bentley, 1870), chapter I.
3. R.A. Austen-Leigh, *Austen Papers, 1704–1856* (Spottiswoode, Ballantyne, 1942), pp. 148–9.
4. Henry Austen, 'A Biographical Notice of the Author', preface to vol. 1 of first edition of *Northanger Abbey* and *Persuasion*.
5. J.E. Austen-Leigh, *Memoir*, chapter V.
6. David Cecil, 'Jane Austen's Lesser Works' in *Collected Reports 1949–1965* (Jane Austen Society, 1967), p. 273.
7. R.A. Austen-Leigh, *Austen Papers*, p. 228.

CHAPTER TWO

1. *Mansfield Park*, chapter xlviii.
2. A.M.W. Stirling (ed.), *The Diaries of Dummer: Reminiscences of an old sportsman, Stephen Terry of Dummer* (Unicorn Press, 1934), chapter II.
3. J.E. Austen-Leigh, *Memoir*, chapter III.
4. Letter 1, 9 January 1796, in Deirdre Le Faye, *Jane Austen's Letters*, 3rd edn, 1995. All letters henceforward listed are from this source.

CHAPTER THREE

1. Letter 29, 3 January 1801.
2. Ibid.
3. *Persuasion*, chapter XV.

4. Constance Hill, *Jane Austen: Her Homes and Her Friends* (John Lane, 1902).
5. Letter 19, 17 May 1799.
6. Letter 20, 2 June 1799.
7. R.A. Austen-Leigh, *Austen Papers, 1704–1856* (Spottiswoode, Ballantyne, 1942).
8. Ibid.
9. Letter 36, 12 May 1801.
10. 25 October 1801, Lefroy archive.
11. 19 May 1803, Lefroy archive.
12. 30 April 1803, Lefroy archive.
13. 16 January 1804, Lefroy archive.
14. David Cecil, 'Jane Austen' in *Poets and Story-tellers* (Constable, 1949), p. 116.
15. Caroline Austen, quoted in D. Le Faye, *A Family Record*.

CHAPTER FOUR

1. *Persuasion*, chapter XI.
2. Letter 39, 14 September 1804.
3. Ibid.
4. *Persuasion*, chapter XII.
5. *Jane Austen and Lyme Regis* (Spottiswoode, Ballantyne, 1944), p. 56.
6. Letter 40, 21 January 1805.

CHAPTER FIVE

1. R.A. Austen-Leigh, *Austen Papers, 1704–1856* (Spottiswoode, Ballantyne, 1942), p. 245.
2. Letter 49, 7 January 1807.
3. Letter 60, 24 October 1808.

CHAPTER SIX

1. Caroline Austen, *My Aunt Jane Austen* (Jane Austen Society, 1952; 1991).
2. Lefroy MS, compiled by Anna Lefroy 1855–72.
3. Letter 71, 25 April 1811.
4. Letter 79, 29 January 1813.

Notes

5. Ibid.
6. Letter 80, 4 February 1813.
7. *British Critic*, February 1813.
8. *New Review*, April 1813.
9. M.A. Austen-Leigh, *Personal Aspects of Jane Austen*, 1920.
10. Letter 86, 3 July 1813.
11. Constance Hill, *Jane Austen: Her Homes and Her Friends* (John Lane, 1902).
12. Letter 90, 25 September 1813.
13. Letter 87, 15–16 September 1813.
14. Letter 88, 16 September 1813.
15. Letter 87, 15–16 September 1813.
16. Letter 90, 25 September 1813.

CHAPTER SEVEN

1. Letter 97, 2 March 1814.
2. 'Opinions of Mansfield Park' in Jane Austen's notebook, British Library, MS 41253A.
3. Caroline Austen, *My Aunt Jane Austen* (Jane Austen Society, 1952, 1991).
4. Letter 125 (A), 16 November 1815.
5. Letter 132 (D), 11 December 1815.
6. Letter 132 (A), (?) 21 December 1815.
7. Letter 138 (A), 27 March 1816.
8. Letter 138 (D), 1 April 1816.

CHAPTER EIGHT

1. Letter from Cassandra Austen to Fanny Knight, CEA/1, 20 July 1817.
2. J.E. Austen-Leigh, *Memoir*, chapter I.
3. J.E. Austen-Leigh, *Memoir*, chapter XI.
4. J.E. Austen-Leigh, *Memoir*, chapter I.

CHAPTER NINE

1. Letter 57, 7 October 1808.
2. Letter 109, 18 November 1814.

N o t e s

3. Letter 114, 30 November 1814.
4. Letter 153, 13 March 1817.
5. D. Le Faye, 'Fanny Knight's Diaries: Jane Austen through her Niece's Eyes', Jane Austen Society of North America, *Occasional Papers No. 2*, 1986.
6. Letter 104, 10 August 1814.
7. Letter 107, 9 September 1814.
8. Letter 108, 28 September 1814.
9. Letter 144, 4 September 1816.
10. Letter 146, 16 December 1816.

CHAPTER TEN

1. Letter 153 to Fanny Knight, 13 March 1817.
2. *Pride and Prejudice*, chapter XXII.
3. Ibid.
4. Letter 6, 15 September 1796.
5. *Memoir of Chief Justice Lefroy, by his son, Thomas Lefroy, MA, QC* (Hodges, Foster, Dublin, 1871).
6. Quoted in Letter 11, 17 November 1798.
7 Ibid.
8. J.E. Austen-Leigh, *Memoir*, Chapter II.

CHAPTER ELEVEN

1. J.E. Austen-Leigh, *Memoir*, Chapter I.

POCKET BIOGRAPHIES

This series looks at the lives of those who have played a significant part in our history – from musicians to explorers, from scientists to entertainers, from writers to philosophers, from politicians to monarchs throughout the world. Concise and highly readable, with black and white plates, chronology and bibliography, these books will appeal to students and general readers alike.

Available

Beethoven
Anne Pimlott Baker

Mao Zedong
Delia Davin

Scott of the Antarctic
Michael De-la-Noy

Alexander the Great
E.E. Rice

Sigmund Freud
Stephen Wilson

Marilyn Monroe
Sheridan Morley and
Ruth Leon

Rasputin
Harold Shukman

POCKET BIOGRAPHIES

Forthcoming

Marie and Pierre Curie
John Senior

Ellen Terry
Moira Shearer

David Livingstone
Christine Nicholls

Margot Fonteyn
Alistair Macauley

Winston Churchill
Robert Blake

Abraham Lincoln
H.G. Pitt

Charles Dickens
Catherine Peters

Enid Blyton
George Greenfield